922

THE MESSAGE OF
JOHN PAUL I

ST. PAUL EDITIONS

Reprinted with permission from *L'Osservatore Romano*, English Edition.

The addresses were taken from the following issues:

N. 35 (544) — August 31, 1978
N. 36 (545) — September 7, 1978
N. 37 (546) — September 14, 1978
N. 38 (547) — September 21, 1978
N. 39 (548) — September 28, 1978
N. 40 (549) — October 5, 1978

Library of Congress Catalogue Card Number: 78-73479

The Daughters of St. Paul are an international religious congregation serving the Church with the communications media.

Table of Contents

A Brief Profile
of John Paul I

Albino Luciani was born in Forno di Canale in the diocese of Belluno on October 17, 1912. His family was by no means rich, in fact, his father had to emigrate to Switzerland as a seasonal laborer until he eventually found work as a craftsman in glass at Murano.

The young Luciani entered the Minor Seminary of Feltre, and then later studied philosophy and theology in the Seminary of Belluno. After ordination to the priesthood on July 7, 1935, he moved to Rome where he studied at the Gregorian University and obtained the doctorate in theology with a brilliant thesis on the origin of the soul in the thought of Rosmini.

On his return in 1937 he served as curate, first in his native parish of Forno di Canale and then at Agordo, while at the same time teaching religion in the local technical institute. From 1937 to 1947 he was vice-rector and Professor of Dogmatic and Moral

Theology, Canon Law, and Sacred Art in the Seminary of Belluno. In 1947, while still continuing as a professor in the seminary, he was appointed Pro-Chancellor and then Pro-Vicar General, and eventually Vicar General of the diocese.

As Secretary he prepared the inter-diocesan Synod of Feltre and Belluno in 1947.

As director of the Catechetical Office he organized the Eucharistic Year and Congress of Belluno of 1949, and later recounted his experiences in his book *"Catechesi in bri-ciole"* which has run to six editions in Italy, while a seventh edition has appeared in Columbia. In it he reveals himself as a gifted writer and keen observer, with qualities of conciseness and clarity which later came to be appreciated.

He was named Bishop of Vittorio Veneto in the Consistory of December 15, 1958, and received episcopal ordination in St. Pe-ter's from Pope John XXIII on the following December 27.

The pastoral activity of Albino Luciani produced abundant results. He carried out his mission with equal intensity on the spiritual and charitable planes. Among his chief concerns was the organization of the clergy and of the Catholic associations. These latter he urged to collaborate closely with the bishop.

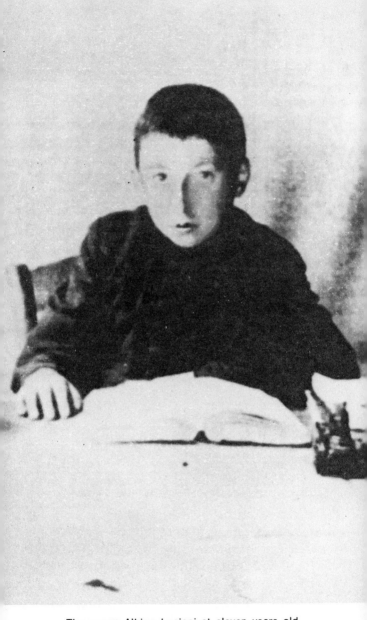

The young Albino Luciani at eleven years old.

As a young student.

GIFT OF CLARITY

His innate clarity of expression came to his aid long years ago when the young Don Albino had to expound the Gospel to the simple folk of his native village. To make himself better understood, he began to insert stories and anecdotes in his short sermons. This style is again evident in a series of "letters" which he published for three years in the monthly "Messaggero di S. Antonio," and which were later gathered into a book. They were addressed to the most diverse characters of history, fable, or literature.

He took part in the Second Vatican Council and was among the most solicitous in having its directives put into effect by issuing opportune instructions to the clergy and faithful of the diocese.

On April 18, 1962, he wrote a pastoral letter ("Notes on the Council") in which he set out a schema of instructions on the Council to be delivered to the faithful. The schema followed the customary form: on the nature of the Council, the various phases of preparation, the scope or purpose of the Council, namely, the solution of doctrinal and practical problems, with an invitation to ecumenical union and an exhortation to prayer and hope.

He made a meticulous study of the subject of responsible parenthood and engaged in consultations and talks with medical specialists and theologians. He warned of the grave responsibility of the Church (the ecclesiastical magisterium) in pronouncing on such a delicate and controverted question.

With the publication of the encyclical *Humanae Vitae,* there could no longer be room for doubt, and the bishop of Vittorio Veneto was among the first to circulate it, and to insist with those who were perplexed by the document that its teaching was beyond question.

Paul VI called him to succeed Cardinal Urbani as Patriarch of Venice on December 15, 1969, but in a sign of humility he did not take possession of the See until February 3, 1970. It was an unforgettable occasion. The whole city was in festive array as Venice received her new pastor as a great gift from the Pope.

A SIMPLE
AND VERY ACTIVE LIFE

The simplicity of the new Patriarch won him the sympathy of all. The long vacancy of the See showed things in a different light and increased the urgency of certain problems.

Venice, where everything seemed tranquil, felt in fact the spiritual ferment of those years, filtered by a spirit traditionally critical and reflective.

Then there was industrial Venice, and it was this that largely engaged the attention of the new Patriarch from the first years of his mission. The development of the Venetian hinterland led to the increase of the families of workers who required priests and churches; on the other hand, there proceeded relentlessly the depopulation of the lagoon area.

Albino Luciani experienced all these worries, and he set to work at once among his people. His example was that of a simple and very active life. For his entrance into the diocese he abolished the traditional pomp and ceremony of the procession of gondolas down the canal to St. Mark's. He walked through the streets, among the people, just like anyone else; he greeted everyone and was always available.

When Paul VI went to Venice in September, 1972, he found a very different city. The gift of the stole by the Pope to the Patriarch in the presence of the huge crowd that thronged St. Mark's Square was interpreted as the announcement of the Red Hat which Pope Paul would confer on him a few months later.

In the Consistory of March 5, 1973, the Pope announced the names of thirty-nine new Cardinals, and among them was Albino Luciani of the Title of St. Mark at Piazza Venezia.

The activity of Cardinal Luciani became much more intense, and his commitments more numerous. In 1971 he took part in the Synod of Bishops, having been invited personally by the Pope. In 1972 he was Vice-President of the Italian Episcopal Conference, an office he held for three years.

At the time of the referendum on divorce in Italy, rather than tolerate the members of FUCI (Federation of Italian Catholic University Students) and of the student community of San Trovaso campaigning in support of divorce, he suppressed both organizations in his diocese, thereby causing a sensation throughout the country. On matters of faith and of Catholic doctrine he was intransigent.

The pastoral appeals to the "critical or dissenting Catholics" increased. They were appeals to the sense of clarity, to the mind of the Church. To place man, instead of God, at the center is not Christianity; for the first commandment is to love God; to love the brethren is the sign of the love for God.

Pluralism may be found in the field of what is open to opinions, but not in that of dogma. Otherwise it becomes a "deadly snare" and an "alteration of the faith."

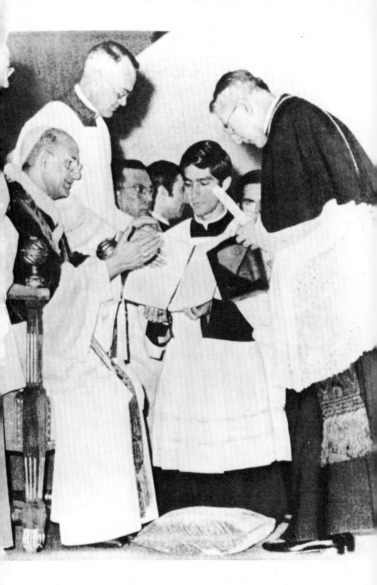

On March 5, 1973, Pope Paul VI consecrated Albino Luciani as a Cardinal.

On two solemnities — the Immaculate Conception (December 8) and the feast of St. Lucy (December 13) — the Patriarch of Venice illustrated to the faithful in St. Mark's the two themes of great doctrinal interest today: "the sacred pluralism" and "the false pluralism."

It is a careful and exhaustive illustration, strewn with stories and examples, with frequent appeals to the Gospel, to the Council, to the words of the Pope. "Sacred pluralism must coexist with the love of the Church and with the authentic mind of the Church.... A healthy pluralism is respectful of the worth of tradition." It is the thought upon which Paul VI had insisted when speaking in the Basilica of St. Mark and appealing "to the goodness and wisdom of the Venetian people."

SERENITY AND BALANCE

On October 25, 1973, Patriarch Luciani opened the twenty-ninth academic year of Theological Study for Laity. He there recalled how the Study hoped to offer a Christian view of life and the modern problems by helping to form a post-conciliar laity, capable of taking with competence its proper place in the People of God, with a faith more enlightened, responsible and mature. Above all, he noted how it offered the contents of the message of salvation in an organic and living treatment comprising the chief theological disciplines, revised and arranged in the light of Vatican II.

At the end of the seventh Rezzara Meeting on September 16, 1974, at Recoaro, Cardinal Luciani gave a masterly discourse on "Populations, environments and resources in international dynamics." Among other points, he indicated that the world resources were not being sufficiently well used if one did not endeavor to improve the quality of the environment for the benefit of the men of today and of tomorrow. Man has the technical power to change the human environment in a thousand ways; it is necessary that the world created by man should not harm that created by God.

Never abandoning his talent as a keen and fresh writer, he published, in "Il Gazzettino" of Venice, an article entitled: "Divorce, a Sacrament in Reverse." There he wrote: "I consider that matrimonial love is the gift of oneself to the other partner; but it is so intimate and noble, so loyal and trusting, that on the one hand it claims everything while on the other hand it excludes everything. Such a love is a decapitated love if it admits of reservations, of provisos and of annulment. The result is that divorce is a sword of Damocles hanging over conjugal love: it generates uncertainty, fear, suspicion. Also, motherhood arouses fears."

Faithful to the principles of the magisterium, he was ready to pardon the sins of the flesh but not those of the spirit. He showed himself particularly severe towards those who have the responsibility to spread their thought in words and in writings, even if such people are in positions of authority.

In an article which appeared in *L'Osservatore Romano* of January 23, 1974, the Patriarch of Venice expressed his mind on "The Responsibility of Theologians." There he emphasized the fact that theologians can exaggerate in the use of their liberty if they forget that theology is a sacred science and treat it as though it were merely one of so many human sciences. They are lacking in fidelity if they concern themselves merely to produce original "discoveries" and to procure glory for themselves, if they forget the good of the Church, if they do not remember that they also run the risk of making gross blunders.

In another article, he discussed the question of "the identity of the priest." The future Pope set about the question as follows:

"I hear it said: 'The priest has lost his identity card.' This is not so .... Let us not lose too much time in asking ourselves who we are, for our priesthood is handled not so much by defining it as by living it. The example of Christ is before us: He was meek and humble, chaste, poor, and obedient. He prayed intensely, keeping in continual contact with the Father, and He taught us to pray. For Him it was so important to be a teacher, a gentle, popular teacher; of Him the listeners were able to say: 'Never has man spoken as this man.'"

Cardinal Luciani always showed himself a Father and vigilant Pastor, even when it was a question of taking up unpopular policies. For the remainder, he used to say with St. Paul: "If I wanted to please men, I would not be a servant of Christ."

His love for his diocese displayed itself in constant and patient work. His meetings with the children in the parishes, in the schools, in the institutes, his simple and friendly lifestyle aroused a deep affection in the faithful. His contacts with the civil authorities were frequent and forceful in support of an improvement in social life.

Cardinal Luciani's activity was always marked by a balance which was the product of interior clarity and serenity. Clarity in his interventions on abortion, in his judgments on movements such as "feminism," and on marxist ideology; clarity and deep study in evaluating phenomena such as violence, terrorism. Only for the assassination of Aldo Moro did he unleash sorrow and

"...The example of Christ is before us: He was meek and humble, chaste, poor and obedient. He prayed intensely, keeping in continual contact with the Father, and He taught us to pray. For Him it was so important to be a teacher, a gentle, popular teacher."

John Paul I

indignation, which he expressed in a pastoral message. "Cruel, cynical and terrifying," he described this deed. "We are crushed, constrained to live in the midst of fear, insecurity, intimidation. Even the least traces of human compassion and fear of God are lacking."

Named bishop by Pope John, and like him Patriarch of Venice, Albino Luciani took up the post of Supreme Pontiff in line with both Pope John and Pope Paul VI. This would seem to be indicated by the name that he chose as Pope—John Paul I.

From the Program of Pope John Paul I

To the Cardinals and to the world, August 27, 1978.

Dear Brothers!
My dear sons and daughters throughout the entire Catholic world!

Having been called by the mysterious and paternal goodness of God to this awesome responsibility of the papacy, we extend to you our greetings. At the same time we greet everyone in the world, all who hear us. Following the teachings of the Gospel, we would wish to think of you as friends, as brothers and sisters. To all of you, we wish good health, peace, mercy and love: "May the grace of our Lord Jesus Christ and the love of God, and the fellowship of the Holy Spirit, be with you all."

We are still overwhelmed at the thought of this tremendous ministry for which we have been chosen: as Peter, we seem to have stepped out on treacherous waters. We are battered by a strong wind. So we turn towards Christ, saying: "Lord, save me" (Mt. 14:30).

Again we hear His voice, encouraging and at the same time lovingly reminding us: "Why do you doubt, oh you of little faith?" If human forces alone cannot be adequate to the task before us, the help of almighty God who has guided His Church throughout the centuries in the midst of great conflicts and opposition will certainly not desert us, this humble and most recent servant of the *servants of God*. Placing our hand in that of Christ, leaning on Him, we have now been lifted up to steer that ship which is the Church; it is safe and secure, though in the midst of storms, because the comforting, dominant presence of the Son of God is with it. According to the words of St. Augustine, an image dear to the ancient Fathers of the Church, the ship of the Church must not fear, because it is guided by Christ and by His Vicar: "Although the ship is tossed about, it is still a ship. It carries the disciples and it receives Christ. Yes, it is tossed on the sea but without it, one would immediately perish" (*Sermon* 75, 3; *PL* 38, 475). Only in the Church is salvation: *without it one perishes!*

We proceed then in this faith. God's assistance will not be wanting to us, just as He has promised: "I am with you always, even to the end of the world" (Mt. 28:20). The common response and willing cooperation of all of you will make the weight of our daily burden lighter. We gird ourself for this awesome task, realizing the uniqueness of the Catholic Church. Its tremendous spiritual power is the guarantee of peace and order; as such it is present in the world; as such it is recognized in the world. The echo of its daily life gives witness that, despite all obstacles, it lives in the heart of men, even those who do not share its truth or accept its message. As the Second Vatican Council (to whose teachings we wish to commit our total ministry as priest, as teacher, as pastor) has said: "Destined to extend to all regions of the earth, the Church enters into human history, though it transcends at once all time and all racial boundaries. Advancing through trials and tribulations, the Church is strengthened by God's grace, promised to her by the Lord so that she may not waver from perfect fidelity, but remain the worthy bride of the Lord, until, through the cross, she may attain to that light which knows no setting" (*Lumen Gentium*, n. 9).

WITNESS OF FAITH

According to God's plan: "All those who in faith look towards Jesus, the Author of salvation and the principle of unity and peace, God has gathered together and established as the Church, that it may be for each and everyone the visible sacrament of this saving unity" *(ibid)*.

In that light we place ourselves interiorly, putting all of our physical and spiritual strength at the service of the universal mission of the Church, that is to say, at the service of the world. In other words, we will be at the service of truth, of justice, of peace, of harmony, of collaboration within nations as well as rapport among peoples. We call especially on the children of the Church to understand better their responsibility: "You are the salt of the earth...you are the light of the world" (Mt. 5:13, 14). Overcoming internal tension which can arise here and there, overcoming the temptation of identifying ourselves with the ways of the world or the appeal of easily won applause, we are, rather, united in the unique bond of love which forms the inner life of the Church as also its external order. Thus, the faithful should be ready to give witness of their own faith to the world: "Always be prepared to give a reason for the hope that is in you" (1 Pt. 3:15).

The Church, in this common effort to be responsible and so respond to the pressing problems of the day, is called to give to the world that "strengthening of the spirit" which is so needed and which alone can assure salvation. The world awaits this today: it knows well that the sublime perfection to which it has attained by research and technology has already reached a peak, beyond which yawns the abyss, blinding the eyes with darkness. It is the temptation of substituting for God one's own decisions, decisions that would prescind from moral laws. The danger for modern man is that he would reduce the earth to a desert, the person to an automaton, brotherly love to planned collectivization, often introducing death where God wishes life.

The Church, admiring yet lovingly protesting against such "achievements," intends, rather, to safeguard the world, that thirsts for a life of love, from dangers that would attack it. The Gospel calls all of its children to place their full strength, indeed their life, at the service of mankind in the name of the charity of Christ: "Greater love than this no man has than that he would lay down his life for his friends" (Jn. 15:13). In this solemn moment, we intend to consecrate all that we are and all that we can achieve to this supreme goal. We will do so until our last breath, aware of the task insistently entrusted to us by Christ: "Confirm your brothers" (Lk. 22:32).

He helps then by strengthening us in our difficult challenge. We remember the example of our predecessors, whose lovable gentle ways, bolstered by a relentless strength, provide both the example and program for the papacy. We recall in particular the great lessons of pastoral guidance left by the most recent Popes, Pius XI, Pius XII, John XXIII. With wisdom, dedication, goodness and love of the Church and the world, they have left an indelible mark on our time, a time that is both troubled and magnificent. Most of all the pontifical pastoral plan of Paul VI, our immediate predecessor, has left a strong impression on our heart and in our memory. His sudden death was crushing to the entire world. In the manner of his prophetic style, which marked his unforgettable pontificate, he placed in clear light the extraordinary stature of a great yet humble man. He cast an extraordinary light upon the Church, even in the midst of controversy and hostility, these past fifteen years. Undertaking immense labors, he worked indefatigably and without rest. He extended himself to carry into effect the Second Vatican Council and to seek world peace, the *tranquility of order.*

IMPLEMENTING VATICAN II

Our program will be to continue his; and his in turn was in the wake of that drawn from the great heart of John XXIII.

— We wish to continue to put into effect the heritage of the Second Vatican Council.

Its wise norms should be followed out and perfected. We must be wary of that effort that is generous perhaps but unwarranted. It would not achieve the content and meaning of the Council. On the other hand, we must avoid an approach that is hesitant and fearful — which thus would not realize the magnificent impulse of the renewal and of life.

CHURCH DISCIPLINE

— We wish to preserve the integrity of the great discipline of the Church in the life of priests and of the faithful. It is a rich treasure in history. Throughout the ages, it has presented an example of holiness and heroism, both in the exercise of the evangelical virtues and in service to the poor, the humble, the defenseless. To achieve that, we place a priority on the revision of the two codes of canon law — that of the oriental tradition and that of the Latin tradition — to assure the blessed liberty of children of God, through the solidarity and firmness of juridical structures.

EVANGELIZATION

— We wish to remind the entire Church that its first duty is that of evangelization. Our predecessor, Paul VI, presented the directions for this in his memorable document: animated by faith, nourished by the Word of God, and strengthened by the heavenly food of the Eucharist, one should study every way, seek every means "in season and out of season" (2 Tm. 4:2), to spread the word, to proclaim the message, to announce that salvation which creates in the soul a restlessness to pursue truth and at the same time offers strength from above. If all the sons and daughters of the Church would know how to be tireless missionaries of the Gospel, a new flowering of holiness and renewal would spring up in this world that thirsts for love and for truth.

ECUMENISM

—We wish to continue the ecumenical thrust, which we consider a final directive from our immediate predecessors. We watch with an unchanging faith, with a dauntless hope and with endless love for the realization of that great command of Christ: "That they may all be one" (Jn. 17:21). His heart anxiously beat for this on the eve of His sacrifice on Calvary. The mutual relationships among the churches of the various denominations have made constant and extraordinary advances as anyone can see; yet division remains a cause for concern, and indeed a contradiction and scandal in the eyes of non-Christians and non-believers. We intend to dedicate our prayerful attention to everything that would favor union. We will do so without diluting doctrine but, at the same time, without hesitation.

PEACE

—We wish to pursue with patience but firmness that serene and constructive dialogue that Paul VI had at the base of his plan and program for pastoral action. The principal theme for this was set forth in his great encyclical *Ecclesiam Suam,* namely, that men, as men, should know one another, even those who do not share our faith. We must always be ready to give witness of the faith that is ours and of the mission that Christ has given to us, "that the world may believe" (Jn. 17:21).

—We wish finally to express our support for all the laudable, worthy initiatives that can safeguard and increase peace in our troubled world. We call upon all good men, all who are just, honest, true of heart. We ask them to help build up a dam within their nations against blind violence which can only destroy and sow seeds of ruin and sorrow. So, too, in international life, they might bring men to mutual understanding, to combining efforts that would further social progress, overcome hunger of body and ignorance of the mind and advance those who are less endowed with goods of this earth, yet rich in energy and desire.

UNIVERSAL GREETINGS

Brothers and dearest sons and daughters, in this awesome moment for us, yet a moment enriched by God's promise, we extend our greeting to all of our sons and daughters: we wish we could see all of them face to face, embrace them, give them courage and confidence, while asking for their understanding and prayers for us.

To all, then, our greeting:

— to the Cardinals of the Sacred College, with whom we have shared this decisive hour. We depend upon them now, as we will in the future. We are grateful to them for their wise counsel. We appreciate the strong support that they will continue to offer us, as an extension of their consent which, through God's will, has brought us to the summit of the apostolic office;

— to all the bishops of the Church of God, "each of whom represents his own Church, whereas all, together with the Pope, represent the entire Church in a bond of peace, love and unity" (*Lumen Gentium*, n. 23). and whose collegiality we strongly value. We value their efforts in the guidance of the universal Church both through the synodal structure and through the curial structure in which they share by right according to the norms established;

— to all of our co-workers called to a strict response to our will and thus to an honored activity which brings holiness of life, called to a spirit of obedience, to the works of the apostolate and to a most exemplary love of the Church. We love each of them and we encourage them to stay close to us as they were to our predecessors in proven faithfulness. We are certain to be able to rely on their highly esteemed labors, which will be for us a great joy.

— We salute the priests and faithful of the diocese of Rome, given to us upon our succession to the Chair of Peter and to the unique and singular title of this Roman See "which presides over the whole society of love" (cf. S. Ignat. *Ep. ad Rom.*, Funk 1, 252).

— We salute in a special way the members of our native diocese of Belluno and those who were entrusted to our care at Venice; they are remembered as most beloved sons and daughters, and of them we think now with a sincere longing, conscious of their magnificent work for the Church and of their common commitment to the cause of the Gospel.

— And we embrace all priests — especially parish priests and those dedicated to the direction of souls, often in difficult conditions or genuine poverty, yet radiating the grace of their vocation in their heroic following of Christ, "the pastor of our souls" (1 Pt. 2:25).

— We salute religious men and women, both those in contemplative and active life, who continue to make present in the world a hymn of total commitment to the Gospel ideal; and we ask them to continue to "see well to it that the Church truly shows forth Christ through them with ever-increasing clarity to believers and unbelievers alike" (*Lumen Gentium,* n. 46).

— We salute the entire missionary Church, and we extend to all men and women, who in their outposts of evangelization dedicate themselves to the care of their brothers, our encouragement and our most loving recognition. They should know that, among all who are dear to us, they are the dearest: they are never forgotten in our prayers and thoughts, because they have a privileged place in our heart.

— To the associations of Catholic Action, as also to the variously named movements which contribute with new energy to the renewal of society and the "consecration of the world" as a leaven in the mass (cf. Mt. 13:33)—to them go all support and encouragement, because we are convinced that their work, carried out in collaboration with the hierarchy, is indispensable for the Church today.

—We salute young people, the hope of tomorrow—a better, a healthier, a more constructive tomorrow—that they may know how to distinguish good from bad and, with the fresh energy that they possess, bring about the vitality of the Church and the development of the world.

—We greet the families who are the "domestic sanctuary of the Church" (*Apostolicam Actuositatem*, n. 11), and indeed a true, actual "domestic Church" (*Lumen Gentium*, n. 11), in which religious vocations can flourish and holy decisions be made. It is there that one is prepared for the world of tomorrow. We exhort them to oppose pernicious ideologies of hedonism which undermine life, and instead to form strong souls endowed with generosity, balance, dedication to the common good.

—We extend a particular greeting to all who are now suffering: to the sick, to prisoners, to exiles, unemployed, or who have bad fortune in life; to all upon whom restraints are placed in their practice of the Catholic faith, which they cannot freely profess except at the cost of the basic human rights of free men and of willing, loyal citizens. In a special way our thoughts turn to the tortured land of Lebanon, to the situation in the homeland of Jesus, to the area of Sahel, to India, a land that is so tried — indeed, to all those sons, daughters, brothers and sisters who undergo privations in their social and political life or as a result of natural disasters.

A DAWN OF HOPE

My brothers and sisters — all people of the world!

We are all obliged to work to raise the world to a condition of greater justice, more stable peace, more sincere cooperation. Therefore we ask and beg all — from the humblest, who are the connective fibers of nations, to heads of state responsible for each nation — to work for a new order, one more just and honest.

A dawn of hope spreads over the earth, although it is sometimes touched by sinister merchants of hatred, bloodshed, and war with a darkness which sometimes threatens to obscure the dawn. This humble Vicar of Christ, who begins his mission in fear yet in complete trust, places himself at the

"We extend our greeting to all of our sons and daughters: we wish we could see all of them face to face, embrace them, give them courage and confidence, while asking for their understanding and prayers for us."

John Paul I

disposal of the entire Church and all civil society. We make no distinction as to race or ideology but seek to secure for the world the dawn of a more serene and joyful day. Only Christ could cause this dawn of a light which will never set, because He is the "sun of justice" (cf. Mal. 4:2). He will indeed oversee the work of all. He will not fail us.

We ask all our sons and daughters for the help of their prayers, for we are counting on them; and we open ourselves with great trust to the assistance of the Lord, who, having called us to be His representative on earth, will not leave us without His all-powerful grace. Mary most holy, Queen of the Apostles, will be the shining star of our pontificate. St. Peter, the foundation of the Church (S. Ambrose, *Exp. Ev. sec. Lucan,* IV, 70: CSEL 32, 4, p. 175), will support us through his intercession and with his example of unconquerable faith and human generosity. St. Paul will guide us in our apostolic efforts directed to all the people of the earth. Our holy patrons will assist us.

In the name of the Father and of the Son and of the Holy Spirit, we impart to the world our first, most loving apostolic benediction.

"I Must Seek To Serve the Church"

Angelus Message, August 27, 1978.

Yesterday morning I went to the Sistine Chapel to vote tranquilly. Never could I have imagined what was about to happen. As soon as the danger for me had begun, the two colleagues who were beside me whispered words of encouragement. One said: "Courage! If the Lord gives a burden, He also gives the strength to carry it." The other colleague said: "Don't be afraid; there are so many people in the whole world who are praying for the new Pope." When the moment of decision came, I accepted.

Then there was the question of the name, for they also ask what name you wish to take, and I had thought little about it. My thoughts ran along these lines: Pope John had decided to consecrate me himself in St. Peter's Basilica; then, however unworthy, I succeeded him in Venice on the Chair of St. Mark, in that Venice which is still full of Pope John. He is remembered by the gondoliers, the sisters, everyone.

Then Pope Paul not only made me a Cardinal, but some months earlier, on the wide footbridge in St. Mark's Square, he made me blush to the roots of my hair in the presence of 20,000 people, because he removed his stole and placed it on my shoulders. Never have I blushed so much!

Furthermore, during his fifteen years of pontificate this Pope has shown, not only to me but to the whole world, how to love, how to serve, how to labor and to suffer for the Church of Christ.

For that reason I said: "I shall be called John Paul." I have neither the "wisdom of the heart" of Pope John, nor the preparation and culture of Pope Paul, but I am in their place. I must seek to serve the Church. I hope that you will help me with your prayers.

On Naming Cardinal Villot as Secretary of State

Letter to Cardinal Villot, August 27, 1978.

To Our Venerable Brother, His Eminence Cardinal Jean Villot, Titular Bishop of the Suburban See of Frascati:

Your Eminence,

Called by the Lord's will, manifested to us through the agreement of the Cardinals, to guide the rudder of the barque of Peter, faced with the formidable responsibility of the pontifical ministry, we are immediately preoccupied about the choice of the one whose duty it would be to be associated more directly in the day-to-day cares of the Church government in the function of Secretary of State.

One's thought immediately turns to you, venerable Brother, to whom our predecessor of venerated memory, Paul VI, had already confided that onerous charge, emphasizing "the gifts of mind, of heart, of will, as also of pastoral awareness and wisdom" (Autograph Letter dated May 2, 1969) for which you are distinguished.

We are pleased, therefore, to entrust to you the office of our Secretary of State, in this way testifying to you in front of the Catholic Episcopate and the whole Church the deep admiration, the sincere appreciation, and the paternal good will that we nourish for you personally. With this our Autograph Letter, we likewise nominate you Prefect of the Council for the Public Affairs of the Church, President of the Pontifical Commission for the Vatican State, and President of the Administration of the Patrimony of the Apostolic See.

We are certain that, thanks to the aid of Him who "does not disappoint those who trust in him" (cf. Dn. 3:40), you, Your Eminence, will know how to cooperate with our pastoral work, sharing with us the day-to-day toil of the apostolic service for building up the Body of Christ, which is the Church (cf. Col. 1:24), for the well-being of all mankind.

Invoking upon you, and upon the work which awaits you, the abundance of heavenly favors, we are happy to convey to you, with the expression of our affection, our strengthening apostolic blessing.

From the Vatican Apostolic Palace, August 27, 1978, the first year of our pontificate.

A Sign and Instrument of Unity

To the Sacred College of Cardinals, August 30, 1978.

Venerable Brothers,

It is with great joy that we see you gathered around us for this meeting which we have earnestly desired. Now, thanks to your courtesy, we are allowed to experience its delight and comfort. In fact, we have felt the impelling need not merely to renew the expression of our gratitude for the choice reserved by you for our humble person — this indeed does not cease to surprise and confuse us — but likewise to testify to the trust that we have in your fraternal and assiduous collaboration. The load which the Lord, in the inscrutable designs of His providence, has willed to place on our weak shoulders would indeed appear to be too weighty if we were not able, in addition to the omnipotent power of His grace, to count upon the affectionate understanding and the active solidarity of brothers so illustrious for doctrine and wisdom, so experienced in pastoral government, so acquainted with the things of God and those of men.

Therefore, let us profit by this occasion to declare that we count first of all on the aid of those eminent Cardinals who will remain near us in this noble city, directing the various departments of which the Roman Curia is made up. The pastoral tasks to which, from time to time, divine Providence called us in previous years were always exercised far away from these complex organisms. These organisms offer to the Vicar of Christ the concrete possibility of carrying out the apostolic service which he owes to the whole Church. They ensure in that organic way the exercise of legitimate autonomies, yet in the indispensable respect of the essential unity of discipline, as well as that of faith, for which Christ prayed on the very eve of His passion (cf. Jn. 17:11, 21-23).

It is not difficult to recognize our inexperience in so delicate a sector of Church life. We promise therefore to treasure the suggestions that will come to us from our worthy co-workers. We will be placing ourselves, one might say, in the school of those who through their well-deserved experience and recognition in these matters of great importance deserve our full trust and our appreciative recognition as well.

Next, our thoughts turn to you, venerable Brothers, who will be returning to your dioceses once again to undertake the pastoral care of the churches entrusted to you by the Spirit (cf. Acts 20:28). You are already anticipating the joy of seeing your sons and daughters whom you know so well and love so deeply. This is a joy which will not be ours. The Lord knows the sadness that there is in our heart because of this. Above all though, in His goodness He knows how to temper the sadness of separation with the prospect of a still broader paternal responsibility. He especially comforts us with that inestimable gift of your loving and sincere support. In this, we experience that same response by all the bishops of the world united to this Apostolic See with the strong bond of one communion.

This unity transcends space, ignores racial difference and enriches us with the true values present in diverse cultures. Though peoples differ in geographical location, in language and mentality, through this one communion they become a single great family. How could one but feel a wave of a brightening hope in face of the marvelous spectacle your presence offers to a reflective spirit? It projects one's mind in the direction of the five continents represented in so dramatic and worthy a fashion by you.

Your presence places before us an eloquent image of the Church of Christ. The Catholic unity of this Church so moved the great Augustine and led him to keep in focus the "small branches" of the single particular churches so that they would not detach themselves "from that great tree which is spread throughout the world through the extension of its branches" (*Letter 185 to Boniface,* n. 8, 32). It is for this unity that we know we have been established both as a sign and as an instrument (cf. *Lumen Gentium,* nn. 22, 2; 23, 1). It is our goal to dedicate our total energy to the defense of this unity and indeed its increase. We are encouraged in this by our awareness that we can trust in the enlightened and generous action of each of you as well. We do not intend to restate the great themes of our program which are already known to you. We would only wish to reconfirm in this moment, together with you all, the commitment of our total availability to the guidance of the Spirit for the good of the Church. It was this that each of you promised on the day of your elevation to the Cardinalate, to serve "even to the shedding of your blood."

Venerable Brothers, last Saturday we found ourselves faced with that momentous decision of saying "yes." We knew that this would place on our shoulders the formidable weight of the apostolic ministry. One of you whispered in my ear encouraging words of trust and confidence. It is fitting then for us, having now been made the Vicar of the One who commanded Peter to "con-

During the inauguration Mass on September 3, 1978, the College of Cardinals individually pledged their fidelity to the new Vicar of Christ, Pope John Paul I.

firm your brothers" (Lk. 22:32), it is fitting for us to remind you that you are now to take up your respective ecclesiastical responsibilities with courage, with firm trust. Even in the difficulty of the present hour, we have the ever-present assistance of Christ. He repeats again to us today the words spoken when the darkness of the passion gathered over Him, words spoken to that first group of believers: "Remember, I have overcome the world" (Jn. 16:33).

In the name of Christ and with the pledge of our paternal good will, we impart to you, to your collaborators, and to all the souls who come under your pastoral care, the first fruits of our propitious apostolic blessing.

Peace and Progress for All Peoples

To the Diplomatic Corps, August 31, 1978.

Your Excellencies, ladies and gentlemen,

We warmly thank your worthy spokesman for his words, which were full of deference, or rather of good will and trust. Our first reaction would be to admit to you our embarrassment at these remarks that give us honor and these sentiments that give us comfort. But we are well aware that this homage and this appeal are addressed through us to the Holy See, to its highly spiritual and humane mission, and to the Catholic Church, whose children are particularly desirous to build, together with their brothers and sisters, a more just and harmonious world.

We have not previously had the honor of making your acquaintance. Until now our ministry was limited to the dioceses entrusted to us and to the pastoral duties that this entailed around Vittorio Veneto and Venice. Nonetheless, it was already a sharing in the ministry of the universal Church.

But now, in this See of the Apostle Peter, our mission had indeed become universal and places us in relationship not only with our Catholic sons and daughters but with all peoples, with their qualified representatives, and more particularly with the diplomats of the countries that have established relations on this level with the Holy See. On these grounds we are very happy to receive you here and to tell you of our esteem for you, our trust in you and our understanding of your noble role. We are happy also to greet through you each one of the nations that you represent. We look on each of them with respect and affection, with an ardent desire for their progress and peace. These nations will become still more familiar to us according as we meet not only their bishops and faithful, but also their civil leaders.

Everybody knows how much was achieved in this field of diplomatic relations by our venerated predecessor. During his pontificate the missions of which you are the heads grew in number. We too wish these relations to be ever more cordial and fruitful for the good of your fellow-citizens, for the good of the Church in your countries, and for the good of universal concord. Moreover, the relationships that you can have with each other at the Holy See also serve understanding and peace. We offer you our sincere collaboration in accordance with the means that belong to us.

In the range of diplomatic posts your role here is unique, just as the mission and competence of the Holy See are unique. Obviously we have no temporal goods to exchange, no economic interests to discuss, such as your states have. Our possibilities for diplomatic interventions are limited and of a special character. They do not interfere with purely temporal, technical and political affairs, which are matters for your governments. In this way, our diplomatic missions to your highest civil authorities, far from being a survival from the past, are a witness to our deep-seated respect for lawful temporal power, and to our lively interest in the humane causes that the temporal power is intended to advance. Similarly, you are here, your governments' spokesmen and watchful witnesses of the Holy See's spiritual activity. On both sides there is presence, respect, exchange and collaboration, without confusing the competences.

Our services, consequently, are of two orders. It can be, if we are invited, participation by the Holy See as such, at the level of your governments or of the international entities, in the search for better solutions to the great problems that see at stake detente, disarmament, peace, justice, humanitarian measures and aid, development, etc. Our representatives or delegates take part in that search, as you know, speaking freely and disinterestedly. That is one appreciable form of cooperation or mutual aid that the Holy See has the possibility of contributing, thanks to the international recognition that it enjoys and the representation of the whole of the Catholic world that it ensures. We are ready to continue in this field the diplomatic and international activity already undertaken, to the extent that participation by the Holy See proves desired and fruitful, and is in correspondence with our means.

But our activity at the service of the international community is also—we would say, chiefly—situated on another level, one that could be more specifically called pastoral and which belongs properly to the Church. It is a matter of contributing, through documents and commitments of the Apostolic See and of our collaborators throughout the Church, to forming consciences—chiefly the consciences of Christians but also those of men and women of good will, and through these forming a wider public opinion—regarding the fundamental principles that guarantee authentic civilization and real brotherhood between peoples. These principles are: respect for one's neighbor, for his life and for his dignity, care for his spiritual and social progress, patience and the desire for reconciliation in the fragile building up of peace; in short, all the rights and duties of life in society and international life, as they have been set forth in the Council's Constitution *Gaudium et Spes* and in so many messages by the late Pope Paul VI. Such attitudes, which in the logic of evangelical love the Christian faithful take or should take for their salvation, contribute to the gradual closer transformation of human relationships, the social fabric, and institutions. They help peoples and the international community to ensure more effectively the conditions for the common good and to discover the final meaning of their forward march. They have a civic and political impact. Your countries are trying to build a modern civilization, dedicating to this task efforts that are often ingenious and generous and have our full understanding and encouragement, as long as they are in conformity with the moral laws written by the Creator in the human heart. But we have confidence in God's help. The Holy See will employ all its strength in that work. It also deserves your full interest.

From today on, our most cordial wishes accompany you in the mission that will be yours with us, as it was with Pope Paul VI. And we invoke upon each of you, on your families, on the countries that you represent, and on all the peoples of the world, abundant blessings from the Most High.

Love of Truth With Respect for Human Dignity

To journalists accredited to the Holy See and the audio-visual personnel, September 1, 1978.

Distinguished ladies and gentlemen, dear sons and daughters:

We are happy to welcome a group from the communications world—a group so qualified and indeed so numerous—in this, the first week of our pontificate. You have come to Rome for a dual event which has had deep meaning for the Catholic Church, deep meaning for the whole world: the death of our lamented predecessor, Pope Paul VI, and the recent conclave in which the heavy burden of ecclesial service as the Supreme Pastor has been placed upon our humble, fragile shoulders.

This welcome meeting allows us to thank you for the sacrifices and the hard work that were yours during the month of August as you served the public opinion of the world.

The service you offer is also a most important one as you offer your readers, listeners and viewers the possibility of sharing in these historic events both in their religious significance and in their profound connection with human values and the expectations of today's society. You do so with the speed and immediacy demanded in your responsible, demanding profession.

We wish to thank you most especially for having so effectively presented and having made better known to the world the person, the teaching, the works and examples of Paul VI. In your many dispatches, your wide coverage, just as in the many pictures that you transmitted from Rome, you have tried in a sensitive way to gather together and to communicate the hope of this city, of the Catholic Church and of the entire world — the hope for a new Pastor who would assure the continuity of the mission of Peter.

The sacred heritage left us by the Second Vatican Council and by our predecessors, John XXIII and Paul VI, of happy and holy memory, contains the pledge of a special concern for a frank, honest and effective working together with the communications media, represented so ably by you. It is a promise that we willingly make, realizing that the means of social communication assume in the life of modern man a function that becomes ever more important. We are mindful of the risks of "massing" and "level-ling" that the mass media contain, the consequent threats to the interiority of the individual, to his capacity for personal reflection, and to his objectivity in judgment. But we also are aware of the new and joyous possibility that they offer to the man of today—the possibility of better knowing and of drawing closer together, the possibility of more closely understanding the desire for justice, for peace, for brotherhood, indeed for building up with one another deeper bonds of sharing, of understanding, of solidarity in view of a more just and humane world. We know, in a word, the ideal goal towards which each of you, despite difficulties and illusions, directs your own energy. You wish to arrive through "communication" at a true and satisfying "communion."As you well know, this is the goal towards which the heart of the Vicar of Him who taught us to call God the unique and loving Father of every human being aspires.

Before giving each of you and your families our special blessing—a blessing we wish to extend to your co-workers and the information organizations represented here—whether agencies, newspapers, radio and television—we wish to reassure you of the esteem we have for your profession. We assure you as well of our desire to facilitate your important and difficult mission. We will do so in the spirit of the directives of the conciliar decree *Inter Mirifica* and the pastoral instruction *Communio et Progressio*. When there are special events or the publication of documents of the Holy See that are of greater importance, you will often have to present the Church, to speak about the Church — at times you will have to comment on our humble ministry. We are confident that you will do so with a love of truth and with a respect for human dignity, because such is the scope of every social communications. We would also ask you to be willing to contribute to the safeguarding in today's society of a deep respect for the things of God and for the mysterious relationship between God and each of us. It is this that constitutes the sacred dimension of human reality. Please understand the profound reasons for which the Pope, the Church and its pastors, in accomplishing their apostolic service, will often have to ask for a spirit of sacrifice, of generosity, of renunciation in order to build up a world of justice, of peace and of love. Certain of maintaining in the future the spiritual bond initiated with this meeting, we grant you from the depth of our heart our apostolic blessing.

Honoring the Mother of God

To Joseph Cardinal Ratzinger, September 1, 1978.

To Our Venerable Brother Cardinal of the Holy Roman Church, Joseph Ratzinger, Archbishop of Munich and Freising:

The symphony of praise with which the most Blessed Virgin Mary is customarily honored throughout the world will be more sublimely extolled — as far as one may fore-see — during this month of September in the State of Ecuador, and particularly in the city of Guayaquil. There, in order to complete and terminate the Marian Year that had been proclaimed, a religious Congress from the whole nation will be held in honor of the Mother of God. The memory flourishes there of a similar Congress held in that same city twenty years ago, which for very beautiful ceremonies and for abundance of spiritual fruit is still remarkable.

By a truly wise decision, taking into account the demands and the needs of this age, two documents of the late Roman Pontiff's magisterium are proposed, so that during these celebrations they may be more deeply explored. One of these documents is *Marialis Cultus;* the other is *Evangelii Nuntiandi.* Therefore a double result is expected from this Congress: an increase of genuine piety towards the Mother of God and a greater eagerness to spread in every direction the saving message of Christ.

Indeed, we embrace the people of Ecuador in sincere charity, and desire in some way to participate in these solemnities in order that greater moment and luster may attend them. Wherefore, by these letters, we choose, make, and proclaim you our Legate Extraordinary, committing to you the office of presiding in our name and with our authority at these Marian celebrations. We have no doubt but that you will skillfully and fruitfully fulfill the office accredited to you, because of the richness of sacred doctrine which commends you, and the ardent love for the Mother of Christ and our Mother for which you are known.

Therefore, may the Marian festival of Guayaquil shine forth with a certain new splendor, at which St. Augustine, amazed, exclaimed: "For whose mind suffices to think, whose tongue suffices to declare not only that in the beginning was the Word who had no beginning of being born, but also that the Word was made flesh, choosing a virgin whom He would make His mother, making the mother whom He would preserve a virgin.... What is this? Who would speak? Who would be silent? An astonishing saying: about that which we cannot speak we are not permitted to remain silent, by crying out we preach that which we cannot comprehend by thought" (Serm. 215, 3; *PL* 38, 1073).

We hope and beseech God that these solemnities may profitably overflow in the life of each man and of society. To you, venerable Brother, as also the sharer of your dignity, Cardinal of the holy Roman Church, Paul Muñoz Vega, who with his assistants undertook many anxieties in preparing this Congress, to the other prelates, public officials, priests, religious, and faithful who for that purpose will be congregated there, we gladly bestow the apostolic blessing, the token of heavenly gifts.

Given at St. Peter's, Rome, on the first day of September, in the year 1978, the first of our pontificate.

More Prayers
and Fewer Battles

Angelus Message, September 3, 1978.

Up there in Veneto I heard it said: every good thief has his devotion. The Pope has a number of devotions; among others, to St. Gregory the Great, whose feast falls to-day. In Belluno the seminary is called Gregorian in honor of St. Gregory the Great. I spent seven years there as a student and twenty as a teacher. It so happens that today, September 3, he was elected Pope and I am officially beginning my service of the universal Church. He was a Roman, who became the first Magistrate of the city. Then he gave everything to the poor, entered a monastery, and became the Pope's secretary. On the Pope's death, he was elected and he did not want to accept. The Emperor, the people, intervened. Afterwards, he finally accepted and wrote to his friend Leandro, Bishop of Seville: "I feel like weeping more than talking." And to the Emperor's sister: "The Emperor has wanted a monkey to become a lion." One sees that in those times, too, it was difficult to be Pope. He was so good to the poor; he converted England. Above all he wrote beautiful books; one is the *Pastoral Rule:* it teaches bishops their trade, but, in the last part, it has the following words: "I have described the good shepherd but I am not one. I have shown the shore of perfection at which to arrive, but personally I am still in the breakers of my faults and my shortcomings, and so please," he said, "so that I will not be shipwrecked, throw me a safety belt with your prayers." I say the same; yet it is not just the Pope who needs prayers, but the world. A Spanish writer has written: "the world is going wrong because there are more battles than prayers." Let us try to see that there may be more prayers and fewer battles.

"Our Presiding
in Charity
Is Service"

*Homily given on the day of the inauguration. of His
Holiness' ministry as Supreme Pastor of the Catholic
Church, September 3, 1978.*

Venerable brothers and dear sons and
daughters,

In this sacred celebration inaugurating
the ministry of the Supreme Pastor of the
Church, which has been placed on our shoulders, we begin by turning our mind in adora-
tion and prayer to the infinite and eternal
God, who has raised us to the Chair of blessed Peter by His own design, which human
reasoning cannot explain, and by His benign
graciousness. The words of St. Paul the
Apostle come spontaneously to our lips: "O
the depth of the riches and wisdom and
knowledge of God! How unsearchable are
his judgments and how inscrutable his
ways!" (Rom. 11:33)

Next we embrace in thought and greet
with paternal affection the whole Church

of Christ. We greet this assembly, representing as it were the whole Church, which is gathered in this place—a place filled with works of piety, religion, and art, which is the attentive custodian of the tomb of the Chief of the Apostles. We then greet the Church that is watching us and listening to us at this moment through the modern media of social communication.

We greet all the members of the People of God: the Cardinals, bishops, priests, men and women religious, missionaries, seminary students, lay people engaged in the apostolate and in various professions, people involved in the fields of politics, culture, art, and business, fathers and mothers of families, workers, migrants, young people, children, the sick, the suffering, the poor.

We greet also with reverence and affection all the people in the world. We regard them and love them as our brothers and sisters, since they are children of the same heavenly Father and brothers and sisters in Christ Jesus (cf. Mt. 23:8ff.).

We have begun this homily in Latin, because, as is well known, it is the official language of the Church and in an evident and effective way expresses its universality and unity.

The Word of God that we have just been listening to has presented the Church to us as in crescendo, first, as prefigured and glimpsed by the Prophet Isaiah (cf. Is. 2:2-5) in the form of the new temple with the nations streaming towards it from all sides, anxious to know the law of God and to observe it with docility, while the terrible weapons of war are transformed into instruments of peace. But St. Peter reminds us that this mysterious new temple, the pole of attraction for the new humanity, has a cornerstone, a living, chosen and precious cornerstone (cf. 1 Pt. 2:4-9), which is Jesus Christ, who founded His Church on the apostles and built it on blessed Peter, their leader (cf. Dogmatic Constitution *Lumen Gentium*, n. 19).

"You are Peter, and on this rock I will build my church" (Mt. 16:18) are the weighty, great and solemn words that Jesus speaks to Simon, son of John, after his profession of faith. This profession of faith was not the product of the Bethsaida fisherman's human logic or the expression of any special insight of his or the effect of some psychological impulse; it was rather the mysterious and singular result of a real revelation of the Father in heaven. Jesus changes Simon's name to Peter, thus signifying the conferring of a special mission. He promises to build on him His Church, which will not be overthrown by the forces of evil or death. He grants him the keys of the kingdom of God, thus appointing him the highest official of His Church, and gives him the power to interpret authentically the law of God. In view of these privileges, or rather these superhuman tasks entrusted to Peter, St. Augustine points out to us: "Peter was by nature simply a man, by grace a Christian, by still more abundant grace one of the apostles and at the same time the first of the apostles" (St. Augustine, *In Ioannis Evang. tract.*, 124, 5: *PL* 35, 1973).

With surprised and understandable trepidation, but also with immense trust in the powerful grace of God and the ardent prayer of the Church, we have agreed to become Peter's successor in the See of Rome, taking on us the yoke that Christ has wished to place on our fragile shoulders. We seem to hear as addressed to us the words that St. Ephraem represents Christ as speaking to Peter: "Simon, my apostle, I have made you the foundation of the holy Church. I have already called you Peter because you will support all the edifices. You are the superintendent of those who will build the Church on earth.... You are the source of the fountain from which my doctrine is drawn. You are the head of my apostles.... I have given you the keys of my kingdom" (St. Ephraem, *Sermones in hebdomadum sanctam*, 4, 1: Lamy T.J., *S. Ephraem Syri hymni et sermones*, 1, 412).

From the moment we were elected, throughout the days that followed, we were deeply struck and encouraged by the warm manifestations of affection given by our sons and daughters in Rome and also by those sending us from all over the world the expression of their irrepressible jubilation at the fact that God has again given the Church her visible Head. Our mind re-echoes spontaneously the emotion-filled words that our great saintly predecessor, St. Leo the Great, addressed to the faithful of Rome: "Blessed Peter does not cease to preside over his See. He is bound to the eternal Priest in an unbroken unity.... Recognize, therefore, that all the demonstrations of affection that you have given me because of fraternal amiability or filial devotion have with greater devotedness and truth been given by you and me to Him whose See we rejoice to serve rather than preside over it" (St. Leo the Great, *Sermo* V, 4-5: *PL* 54, 155-156).

Yes, our presiding in charity is service. In saying this, we think not only of our Catholic brothers and sons and daughters but also of all those who endeavor to be disciples of Jesus Christ, to honor God, and to work for the good of humanity.

In this way we greet affectionately and with gratitude the delegations from other Churches and ecclesial communities present here. Brethren not yet in full communion, we turn together to Christ our Savior, advancing all of us in the holiness in which He wishes us to be and also in the mutual love without which there is no Christianity, preparing the paths of unity in faith, with respect for His truth and for the ministry that He entrusted, for His Church's sake, to His apostles and their successors.

Furthermore, we owe a special greeting to the heads of state and the members of the Extraordinary Missions. We are deeply touched by your presence, you who preside over the high destinies of your countries, or represent your governments or international organizations, for which we are most grateful. In your participation we see the esteem and trust that you place in the Holy See and the Church, that humble messenger of the Gospel for all the peoples of the earth, in order to help create a climate of justice, brotherhood, solidarity and hope, without which the world would be unable to live.

Let all here, great or small, be assured of our readiness to serve them according to the Spirit of the Lord.

Surrounded by your love and upheld by your prayers, we begin our apostolic service by invoking, as a resplendent star on our way, the Mother of God, Mary — *Salus Populi Romani,* and *Mater Ecclesiae* — whom

the liturgy venerates in a special way in this month of September. May our Lady, who guided with delicate tenderness our life as a boy, as a seminarian, as a priest and as a bishop, continue to enlighten and direct our steps, in order that, as Peter's voice and with our eyes and mind fixed on her Son Jesus, we may proclaim in the world with joyous firmness our profession of faith: "You are the Christ, the Son of the living God" (Mt. 16:16). Amen.

In the Service of Justice To Build Peace

To the special missions present for inauguration of the Pontificate, September 4, 1978.

Your Excellencies, ladies and gentlemen,

During the celebration yesterday, we were able to address to you only a short greeting. Today, we are anxious to tell you the joy, emotion and honor which your participation in the opening of our pontificate brought us. We owe you very deep gratitude — to yourselves in the first place, and to the countries or international organizations which you represent.

This homage of so many nations is very fine and very encouraging. Not that our person deserved it: yesterday we were only a priest and a bishop of an Italian province, dedicating all his strength and his talents to the apostolate entrusted to him. And now today we are called to the See of the Apostle Peter. We inherit his great mission with regard to all nations, the one he received by pure grace from the hands of our Lord Jesus Christ, who according to the Christian faith is the Son of God and Savior of the world. We often think of this sentence of the Apostle Paul: "But we have this treasure in earthen vessels, to show that the transcendent power belongs to God and not to us" (2 Cor. 4:7). Fortunately, too, we are not alone: we act in communion with the bishops of the Catholic Church all over the world.

What delights us, therefore, is that beyond the good will shown to our person, your homage signifies in our eyes the permanent and fascinating attraction that the Gospel and the things of God keep in our universe. It expresses the esteem and trust that nearly all peoples cherish for the Church and the Holy See, for their multiform activities, in the specifically spiritual field as in the service of justice, development and peace. It must be added that the action of the recent Popes, in particular our venerated predecessor Paul VI, made a great contribution to this international influence.

As for us, we are ready to continue this disinterested work, according to our possibilities, and to sustain our collaborators engaged in it. Even if we do not know all your countries personally, and unfortunately cannot speak to you in each of your mother tongues, our heart is completely open to all peoples and to all races. We hope that each one may find his place in the concert of nations and develop the gifts that God has given him in peace, and thanks to the understanding and solidarity of others. Nothing that is really human will be alien to us. Certainly, we do not have miracle-solutions for the great world problems. We can, however, bring something very precious: a spirit which helps to unravel these problems and sets them along the course which is essential, that of universal charity and opening to transcendent values, that is, opening to God. We will try to carry out this service in simple, clear and trustful language.

Allow us in our turn to rely on your benevolent collaboration. We hope in the first place that Christian communities will always enjoy, in your country, the respect and freedom to which every religious conscience is entitled, and that their contribution in the pursuit of the common good will be given a just place. We are sure, too, that you will continue to receive favorably the initiatives of the Holy See, when the latter proposes to serve the international community, to recall the requirements of a wholesome life in society, and to defend the rights and the dignity of all men, particularly the humble and minorities.

Thank you again for your visit. We willingly invoke God's assistance on yourselves, your families and one and all of your countries and the world organizations which you represent. In the greatest responsibilities, may God keep our minds lucid and our hearts in peace!

Sympathy on the Death of Metropolitan Nikodim

Saddened by the death of the Metropolitan of Leningrad, His Eminence Nikodim, which occurred unexpectedly on the morning of September 5, during the audience to the delegations of non-Catholic Christian Churches and Communities, His Holiness Pope John Paul I sent the following telegram to the Patriarch of Moscow, His Holiness Pimen:

His Holiness PIMEN
Patriarch of Moscow and
of all Russia
18-2 Rue Ryleev
Moscow 119034 USSR

Deeply moved by the death of the Metropolitan Nikodim, which occurred as we were conversing with him, we express to Your Holiness and to the Holy Synod of the Russian Orthodox Church our feelings of keen sorrow. We assure you of our prayer for the repose of the soul of this devoted servant of his Church and constructor of the deepening relations between our Churches. May God receive him into his joy and his peace.

"If human forces alone cannot be adequate to the task before us, the help of almighty God who has guided His Church throughout the centuries in the midst of great conflicts and opposition will certainly not desert us, this humble and most recent servant of the *servants of God*.

"We proceed then in this faith. God's assistance will not be wanting to us, just as He has promised: 'I am with you always, even to the end of the world' (Mt. 28:20)." —John Paul I

"Placing our hand in that of Christ, leaning on Him, we have now been lifted up to steer that ship which is the Church; it is safe and secure, though in the midst of storms, because the comforting, dominant presence of the Son of God is with it."   —John Paul I

"Surrounded by your love and upheld by your prayers, we begin our apostolic service by invoking, as a resplendent star on our way, the Mother of God, Mary...."

"May our Lady, who guided with delicate tenderness our life as a boy, as a seminarian, as a priest and as

a bishop, continue to enlighten and direct our steps, in order that, as Peter's voice and with our eyes and mind fixed on her Son Jesus, we may proclaim in the world with joyous firmness our profession of faith: 'You are the Christ, the Son of the living God' (Mt. 16:16). Amen." —John Paul I

"We call especially on the children of the Church to understand better their responsibility: 'You are the salt of the earth...you are the light of the world' (Mt. 5:13, 14). Overcoming internal tension which can arise here and there, overcoming the temptation of identifying ourselves with the ways of the world or the appeal of easily won applause, we are, rather, united in the unique bond of love which forms the inner life of the Church as also its external order. Thus, the faithful should be ready to give witness of their own faith to the world: 'Always be prepared to give a reason for the hope that is in you ' (1 Pt. 3:15)." —John Paul I

"Let each of us try to be good and to infect others with a goodness imbued with the meekness and love taught by Christ. Christ's golden rule was: 'Do not do to others what you do not want done to yourself. Do to others what you want done to yourself.' And He always gave. Put on the cross, not only did He forgive those who crucified Him, but He excused them. He said: 'Father, forgive them for they know not what they do.' This is Christianity; these are sentiments which, if put into practice, would help society so much." —John Paul I

"...To love God is also a journey: God wants it to be more and more intense and perfect. He said to all His followers: 'You are the light of the world, the salt of the earth' (Mt. 5:13-14); 'You must be perfect as your heavenly Father is perfect' (Mt. 5:48). That means: to love God not a little, but so much; not to stop at the point at which we have arrived, but with His help, to progress in love."

—John Paul I

"If all the sons and daughters of the Church would know how to be tireless missionaries of the Gospel, a new flowering of holiness and renewal would spring up in this world that thirsts for love and for truth."

—John Paul I

"**Our message must be a clear proclamation of salvation in Jesus Christ. With Peter we must say to Christ, in the presence of our people: 'You have the words of eternal life' (Jn. 6:69)."** —John Paul I

(Felici)

Pope John Paul I with Humberto Cardinal Medeiros of Boston, Ma.

The Great Virtue
of Humility

To a General Audience, September 6, 1978.

On my right and on my left there are Cardinals and bishops, my brothers in the episcopate. I am only their elder brother. My affectionate greeting to them and also to their dioceses!

Just a month ago, Paul VI died at Castelgandolfo. In fifteen years he rendered enormous services to the Church. The effects are partly seen now already, but I think that they will be seen especially in the future. Every Wednesday he came here and spoke to the people. At the 1977 Synod several bishops said: "Pope Paul's Wednesday addresses are a real catechesis adapted to the modern world." I will try to imitate him, in the hope that I, too, will be able, somehow, to help people to become better.

To be good, however, it is necessary to be in place before God, before our neighbor and before ourselves. Before God, the right position is that of Abraham, who said: "I am only dust and ashes before you, O Lord!" We must feel small before God. When I say, "Lord, I believe," I am not ashamed to feel like a child before his mother; one believes in one's mother; I believe in the Lord, in what He has revealed to me. The commandments are a little more difficult to observe; but God gave them to us not to satisfy a whim, not in His own interest, but solely in our interest.

Once a man went to buy a motorcar from the agent. The latter talked to him plainly: "Look here, it's a good car; mind that you treat it well; premium petrol in the tank, and for the joints, oil the good stuff." But the other replied: "Oh, no, for your information, I can't stand even the smell of petrol, nor oil; I'll put champagne, which I like so much, in the tank and I'll oil the joints with jam." "Do what you like; but don't come and complain if you end up in a ditch with your car!" The Lord did something similar with us: He gave us this body, animated by an intelligent soul, a good will. He said, "this machine is a good one, but treat it well."

Here are the commandments. Honor your father and your mother; do not kill;

do not get angry; be gentle; do not tell lies;
do not steal.... If we were able to observe
the commandments, we would be better off,
and so would the world. Then there is our
neighbor.... But our neighbor is at three
levels: some are above us; some are at our
level; some are below. Above, there are
our parents. The catechism said: respect
them, love them, obey them. The Pope must
instill respect and obedience in children
for their parents. I am told that the choir-
boys of Malta are here. Let one come here,
please...the choir boys of Malta, who have
served in St. Peter's for a month.

"Well, what is your name?"

"James!"

"James. And listen, have you ever
been ill?"

"No."

"Ah, never?"

"No."

"Never been ill?"

"No."

"Not even a temperature?"

"No."

"Oh, how lucky you are! But when a
child is ill, who brings him a little broth,
some medicine? Isn't it his mother? That's
it. Afterwards you grow up, and your mother
gets old; you become a fine gentleman, and
your mother, poor thing, will be in bed, ill.

That's it. Well, who will bring the mother a little milk and medicine? Who will?"

"My brothers and I."

"Well said! 'His brothers and he,' he said. I like that. Did you understand?"

But it does not always happen. As Bishop of Venice, I sometimes went to homes. Once I found an elderly woman, sick.

"How are you?"

"Well, the food is all right!"

"Are you warm? Is there heating?"

"It's good."

"So you are content?"

"No." She almost began to cry.

"But why are you crying?"

"My daughter-in-law, my son, never come to see me. I would like to see my grandchildren."

Heat and food are not enough, there is the heart; we must think of the heart of our old people. The Lord said that parents must be respected and loved, even when they are old. And besides our parents, there is the state, there are superiors. May the Pope recommend obedience? Bossuet, who was a great bishop, wrote: "Where no one commands, everyone commands. Where everyone commands, no one commands any longer, but chaos." Sometimes something similar is seen in this world too. So let us respect those who are our superiors.

Then there are our equals. And here, there are usually two virtues to observe: justice and charity. But charity is the soul of justice. We must love our neighbor, the Lord recommended it so much. I always recommend not only great acts of charity, but little ones. I read in a book, written by Carnegie, an American, entitled *How To Make Friends,* the following little episode:

A lady had four men in the house: her husband, a brother, two grown-up sons. She alone had to do the shopping, the washing, the ironing and the cooking: everything all alone. One Sunday they come home. The table is laid for dinner, but on the plate there is only a handful of hay. "Oh!" the others protest and say: "What! Hay!" And she says, "No, everything is ready. Let me tell you: I prepare your food; I keep you clean; I do everything. Never once have you said: 'That was a good dinner you made for us.' But say something! I'm not made of stone."

People work more willingly when their work is recognized. These are the little acts of charity. In our home we all have someone who is waiting for a compliment.

There are those who are smaller than we are; there are children, the sick, even sinners. As bishop, I was very close even to those who do not believe in God. I formed the idea that they often combat not God,

"I will just recommend one virtue so dear to the Lord. He said, 'Learn from me who am meek and humble of heart.'"

John Paul I

but the mistaken idea they have of God. How much mercy it is necessary to have! And even those who err.... We must really be in place with ourselves. I will just recommend one virtue so dear to the Lord. He said, "Learn from me who am meek and humble of heart." I run the risk of making a blunder, but I will say it: the Lord loves humility so much that, sometimes, He permits serious sins. Why? In order that those who committed these sins may, after repenting, remain humble. One does not feel inclined to think oneself half a saint, half an angel, when one knows that one has committed serious faults. The Lord recommended it so much: be humble. Even if you have done great things, say: "We are useless servants." On the contrary, the tendency in all of us is rather the opposite: to show off. Lowly, lowly: this is the Christian virtue which concerns ourselves.

For a Just and Full Peace

One of the most significant points made by the Pope at the end of the General Audience on Wednesday, September 6, was the need for prayer to assist the happy outcome of the talks at Camp David. The Holy Father spoke as follows:

Now, if you permit, I should like to invite you to join with me in prayer for an intention that I have much at heart. You have learned from the press, from television, that today at Camp David an important meeting begins between the rulers of Egypt, Israel and the United States, in the hope of finding a solution to the conflict in the Middle East. This conflict, which for more than thirty years has been continued on the land of Jesus, has already caused so many victims, so much suffering, both among the Arabs and the Israeli. Like an evil malady it has infected the neighboring countries.

Think of Lebanon, a martyred Lebanon, up-set by the repercussions of this crisis. For this, then, I should like to pray together with you for the success of the Camp David meeting: that these talks may pave the way towards a full and just peace. Just: that is, to the satisfaction of all the parties in the conflict. Full: without leaving any problem unresolved; the problem of the people of Palestine, the security of Israel, the Holy City of Jerusalem. Let us ask the Lord to enlighten those responsible for all the peoples concerned, so that they may be far-seeing and courageous in making the decisions that should bring serenity and peace to the Holy Land and to the whole world of the East.

Respect for Man's Body and Spirit

During the General Audience, Pope John Paul I had a special word for the members of the Seventh International Congress of the Organ Transplant Society.

We owe a special greeting to members of the Seventh International Congress of the Organ Transplant Society. We are very touched by your visit, which is a homage to the Pope, and particularly by your desire to throw light on and to study more deeply the serious human and moral problems at stake in the researches or in the surgical technique which are your lot. We encourage you, in this field, to request the help of Catholic friends, expert in theology and in morality and with a thorough knowledge of your problems, possessing a sound knowledge of Catholic doctrine and a deeply human understanding.

We are content today to express to you our congratulations and our trust, for the immense work that you put in the service of human life in order to prolong it in better conditions. The whole problem is to act with respect for the person and for one's neighbors, whether it is a question of donors of organs or beneficiaries, and never to transform man into an object of experiment. There is respect for his body; there is also respect for his spirit. We pray to God, the Author of life, to inspire you and assist you in these magnificent and formidable responsibilities. May He bless you, with all your dear ones!

The "Great" Discipline

To the clergy of Rome, September 7, 1978.

I heartily thank the Cardinal Vicar for the good wishes that he addressed to me on behalf of all those present. I know what a faithful and precious help he was to my unforgettable predecessor and I hope he will continue the same collaboration for me. I greet affectionately Monsignor the Vicegerent, the auxiliary bishops, the officials of the various centers and offices of the Vicariate, and then all the individual priests in care of souls within the diocese and its district: the parish priests in the first place, their co-workers, the religious, and, through them, Christian families and the faithful.

ACCORDING TO THE GOSPEL

You may have noted that, already when speaking to the Cardinals in the Sistine Chapel, I mentioned the "great discipline of the Church" to be "preserved in the lives of the faithful." My revered predecessor often spoke on this subject; allow me to talk to you very briefly about it with brotherly familiarity, at this first meeting.

There is the "little" discipline, which is limited to purely external and formal observance of juridical norms. I would like, on the contrary, to speak of the "great" discipline. The latter exists only if external observance is the fruit of deep convictions and the free and joyful projection of a life lived deeply with God. It is a question — Abbé Chautard writes — of the activity of a soul which reacts continually to master its bad inclinations and to acquire, a little at a time, the habit of judging and behaving in all the circumstances of life according to the maxims of the Gospel and the examples of Jesus. "To master inclinations" is discipline. The phrase "a little at a time" indicates discipline, which requires a continued, long, and difficult effort. Even the angels that Jacob saw in a dream were not flying, but climbing one step at a time; you can just imagine us, poor men without wings.

The "great" discipline requires a suitable atmosphere; and, in the first place, meditation. At Milan station I once saw a porter, who, with his head resting on a sack of coal propped against a pillar, was sound asleep.... Trains left whistling and arrived with clanking wheels; the loudspeakers continually boomed out announcements; people came and went in confusion and noise, but he — sleeping on — seemed to be saying: "Do what you like, but I need to be quiet." We priests should do something similar: around us there is continual movement and talking — of persons, newspapers, radio and television. With priestly moderation and discipline we must say: "Beyond certain limits, for me, who am a priest of the Lord, you do not exist. I must take a little silence for my soul. I detach myself from you to be united with my God."

And today it is the desire of many good faithful to feel their priest habitually united with God. They reason like the lawyer of Lyons on his return from a visit to the Curé d'Ars. "What did you see at Ars?" he was asked. Answer: "I saw God in a man." St. Gregory the Great reasons in a similar way. He hopes that the pastor of souls will dialogue with God without forgetting men, and dialogue with men without forgetting God. And he goes on: "Let the pastor avoid the temptation of wishing to be loved by the faithful instead of by God, or of being too weak for fear of losing men's affection;

let him not lay himself open to the divine reproach: 'Woe to those who sew magic bands upon all wrists' (Ez. 13:18)." "The pastor," he concludes, "must indeed try to make himself loved, but in order to win a hearing, not to seek this affection for his own profit" (cf. *Regula Pastoralis*, 1.II, c. VIII).

To a certain degree all priests are guides and pastors; but have they all the right idea of what it really means to be pastor of a particular Church, that is, a bishop? On the one hand, Jesus, the Supreme Pastor, said of Himself: "All authority in heaven and on earth has been given to me" (Mt. 28:19). And on the other hand He added: "I came to serve" (cf. Mt. 20:28), and He washed His apostles' feet. In Him, therefore, power and service went together.

Something similar should be said of the apostles and bishops. "*Praesumus*," Augustine said, "*si prosumus*" (*Miscellanea Augustiniana*, Romae 1930, t. I, p. 565); we bishops preside if we serve: our presidency is just if it consists of service or takes place for the purpose of service, with the spirit and style of service. This episcopal service would be lacking, however, if the bishop did not wish to exercise the powers received. Augustine said further: "The bishop who does not serve the public (by preaching and guidance) is only *foeneus custos* — a scarecrow put in the vineyards so that the birds will not peck the grapes" (*ibid.*, p. 568). For this reason it is written in *Lumen Gentium:* "Bishops govern...by their counsel, exhortations, and example, as well, indeed, as by their authority and sacred power" (*LG* 27/ 351).

PASTORAL SERVICE

Another element of priestly discipline is love of one's own job. It is not easy, I know, to love one's job and stick to it when things are not going right, when one has the impression that one is not understood or encouraged, when inevitable comparisons with the job given to others would drive us to become sad and discouraged. But are we not working for the Lord? Ascetical theology teaches: do not look at whom you obey, but for whom you obey. Reflection helps, too. I have been a bishop for twenty years. On several occasions I suffered because I was unable to reward someone who really deserved it; but either the prize position was lacking or I did not know how to replace the person, or adverse circumstances occurred. Then, too, St. Francis de Sales wrote: "There is no vocation that does not have its troubles, its vexations, its disgust. Apart from those who are fully resigned to God's will, each of us would like to change his own condition with that of others. Those who are bishops wish they were not; those who are married wish they were not, and those who are not married wish that they were. Where does this general restlessness of spirit come from, if not from a certain allergy that we have towards constraint and from a spirit that is not good, which make us suppose that others are better off than we are?" (St. Francis de Sales, *Oeuvres*, edit. Annecy, t. XII, 348-9)

I have spoken simply and I apologize for it. I can assure you, however, that since I have become your bishop I love you a great deal. And it is with a heart full of love that I impart to you the apostolic blessing.

In Prayer Is
the Hope for Peace

Angelus Message, September 10, 1978.

At Camp David, in America, Presidents Carter and Sadat and Prime Minister Begin are working for peace in the Middle East. All men are hungry and thirsty for peace, especially the poor, who pay more and suffer more in troubled times and in wars; for this reason they look to the Camp David meeting with interest and great hope. The Pope, too, has prayed, had prayers said, and is praying that the Lord may deign to help the efforts of these politicians.

I was very favorably impressed by the fact that the three Presidents wished to express their hope in the Lord publicly in prayer. President Sadat's brothers in religion are accustomed to say as follows: "There is pitch darkness, a black stone and on the stone a little ant; but God sees it, and does not forget it." President Carter, who is a fervent Christian, reads in the Gospel: "Knock, and it will be opened to you; ask, and it will be given you. Even the hairs of your head are all numbered." And Premier Begin recalls that the Jewish people once passed difficult moments and addressed the Lord complaining and saying: "You have forsaken us; You have forgotten us!" "No!" — He replied through Isaiah the Prophet — "Can a mother forget her own child? But even if it should happen, God will never forget His people."

Also we who are here have the same sentiments; we are the objects of undying love on the part of God. We know: He always has His eyes open on us, even when it seems to be dark. He is our Father; even more, He is our mother. He does not want to hurt us; He wants only to do good to us, to all of us. If children are ill, they have additional claim to be loved by their mother. And we, too, if by chance we are sick with badness, on the wrong track, have yet another claim to be loved by the Lord.

With these sentiments I invite you to pray together with the Pope for each of us, for the Middle East, for Iran, and for the whole world.

Sympathy on Death of Cardinal Gracias

On hearing of the death of His Eminence Cardinal Valerian Gracias, Archbishop of Bombay, which occurred on Monday, September 11, His Holiness Pope John Paul I sent a telegram of sympathy to Cardinal Picachy, President of the Episcopal Conference of India.

We share the sorrow of the entire Church in India at the death of our beloved brother, Cardinal Valerian Gracias. The memory of his love for Christ and the Gospel will remain an inspiration for future generations of clergy, religious and laity who strive to build up God's kingdom by word and deed. With paternal affection we impart to all who mourn him in Christian hope our special apostolic blessing.

The Holy Father also sent a telegram of sympathy to Archbishop Pimenta, Coadjutor with the right of succession to the late Cardinal Gracias.

We know that the death of Cardinal Gracias is deeply felt by the whole Archdiocese of Bombay. In this hour of sorrow we give the assurance of our prayers for his soul, invoking upon him the joy and peace of new life in Christ. We ask God to confirm all of you in the strength and consolation of Christian hope, and in the love of the Savior we impart our apostolic blessing.

To Live the Faith

To a General Audience, September 13, 1978.

My first greeting goes to my bishop confreres, of whom I see many here.

Pope John, in a note of his, which was also published, said: "This time I gave the retreat on the Seven Lamps of Sanctification." Seven virtues, he meant, that is, faith, hope, charity, prudence, justice, fortitude, temperance. Who knows if the Holy Spirit will help the poor Pope today to illustrate at least one of these lamps, the first one—faith.

Here in Rome there was a poet, Trilussa, who also tried to speak of faith. In a certain poem of his, he said: "That little old blind woman, whom I met / the evening I lost my way in the middle of the wood, / said to me: —If you don't know the way / I'll accompany you, for I know it. / If you have the strength to follow me / from time to time I'll call you, right to the bottom there, where there is a cypress, / right to the top there, where there is a cross. I answered: that may be...but I find it strange / that I can be guided by someone sightless.... / The blind woman, then, took my hand / and sighed: Come on. —It was faith." As a poem, it is delightful; as theology, defective.

It is defective because when it is a question of faith, the great stage manager is God. Because Jesus said: "No one comes to me unless my Father draws him." St. Paul did not have faith, in fact he was persecuting the faithful. God waits for him on the way to Damascus: "Paul," He says to him, "don't take it into your head to rear up, to kick, like a restive horse. I am that Jesus whom you are persecuting. I need you. You must change!" Paul surrendered; he changed, leading a completely different life. Some years afterwards, he will write to the Philippians: "That time, on the way to Damascus, God seized me; since then I have done nothing but run after Him, to see if I, too, am able to seize Him, imitating Him, loving Him more and more."

That is what faith is: to surrender to God, but transforming one's life—a thing

that is not always easy! Augustine has told
of the journey of his faith; especially in the
last few weeks it was terrible; reading, one
feels his soul almost shudder and writhe
in interior conflicts. On the one hand, God
calls him and insists; on the other hand, his
old habits, "old friends," he writes...:
"and they pulled me gently by my mantle
of flesh and they said to me: 'Augustine,
what! You are abandoning us? Look out,
you won't be able to do this any more, you
won't be able ever again to do that other.'"
A hard thing! "I felt," he says, "like one who
is in bed in the morning. He is told: 'Out,
Augustine, get up!' Finally the Lord gave me
a sharp tug, and I came out. You see, one
mustn't say: '*Yes, but; yes, but later.*' One
must say: 'Yes, Lord! At once!' This is faith.
To respond to the Lord generously. But who
says this 'yes'? He who is humble and trusts
God completely!"

My mother used to tell me when I was
a boy: "When you were little, you were very
ill. I had to take you from one doctor to another and watch over you whole nights; do
you believe me?" How could I have said:
"I don't believe you, Mamma"? "Of course
I believe, I believe what you tell me, but I
believe especially in you."

And so it is with faith. It is not just a
question of believing in the things that God
revealed, but in Him who deserves our faith,

who has loved us so much and done so much for our sake.

It is also difficult to accept some truths, because the truths of faith are of two kinds: some pleasant, others unpalatable to our spirit. For example, it is pleasant to hear that God has so much tenderness for us, even more tenderness than a mother has for her children, as Isaiah says. How pleasant and congenial it is! There was a great French bishop, Dupanloup, who used to say to the rectors of seminaries: "With the future priests, be fathers, be mothers." It is agreeable. Other truths, on the contrary, are hard to accept. God must punish, if I resist. He runs after me, begs me to repent and I say: "No!" I almost force Him to punish me. This is not agreeable. But it is a truth of faith. And there is a last difficulty, the Church. St. Paul asked: "Who are you, Lord?" "I am that Jesus whom you are persecuting." A light, a flash, crossed his mind. I do not persecute Jesus, I don't even know Him: I persecute the Christians. It is clear that Jesus and the Christians, Jesus and the Church, are the same thing: indissoluble, inseparable.

Read St. Paul: *"Corpus Christi quod est Ecclesia."* Christ and the Church are only one thing. Christ is the Head, we, the Church, are His limbs. It is not possible to have faith and to say, "I believe in Jesus; I ac-

cept Jesus but I do not accept the Church."
We must accept the Church, as she is. And
what is this Church like? Pope John called her
"Mater et Magistra." Teacher also. St. Paul
said: "Let everyone accept us as Christ's
aides and stewards and dispensers of His
mysteries."

When the poor Pope, when the bishops,
the priests, propose the doctrine, they are
merely helping Christ. It is not our doctrine,
it is Christ's; we must just guard it and
present it. I was present when Pope John
opened the Council on October 11, 1962.
At a certain point he said: "We hope that
with the Council the Church will take a
leap forward." We all hoped so; but a leap
forward, in what way? He told us at once:
on certain and immutable truths. It never
even occurred to Pope John that the truths
could go forward, and then, gradually,
change. Those are the truths; we must walk
along the way of these truths, understanding
them more and more, bringing ourselves up-
to-date, proposing them in a form suited to
the new times. Pope Paul too had the same
thought. The first thing I did, as soon as I
was made Pope, was to enter the private
chapel of the Pontifical Household. Right at
the back Pope Paul had two mosaics made—
St. Peter and St. Paul: St. Peter dying, St. Paul
dying. But under St. Peter are the words of
Jesus: "I will pray for you, Peter, that your

faith may never fail." Under St. Paul, on whom the sword falls: "I have run my race, I have kept the faith." You know that in his last address on June 29, Paul VI said: "After fifteen years of pontificate, I can thank the Lord that I have defended the faith, that I have kept the faith."

The Church is also a mother. If she continues Christ, and Christ is good, the Church too must be good; good to everyone. But if by chance there should sometimes be bad people in the Church? We have our mother. If mother is sick, if my mother by chance should become lame, I love her even more. It is the same in the Church. If there are—and there are—defects and short-comings, our affection for the Church must never fail. Yesterday, and I conclude, I was sent the issue of *"Città Nuova."* I saw that they have reported, recording it, a very short address of mine, with an episode. A certain British preacher, MacNabb, speaking in Hyde Park, had spoken of the Church. When he finished, someone asked to speak and said: "Yours are fine words. But I know some Catholic priests who did not stay with the poor and became rich. I know also Catholic husbands who have betrayed their wives. I do not like this Church made of sinners."

The Father said: "There's something in what you say. But may I make an objection?"

"Let's hear it."

He says: "Excuse me, but am I mistaken or is the collar of your shirt a little greasy?"

He says: "Yes, it is, I admit."

"But is it greasy because you haven't used soap, or because you used soap but it was no use?"

"No," he says, "I haven't used soap."

You see. The Catholic Church too has extraordinary soap: the Gospel, the sacraments, prayer. The Gospel read and lived; the sacraments celebrated in the right way; prayer well used, would be a marvelous soap, capable of making us all saints. We are not all saints, because we have not used this soap enough. Let us try to meet the hopes of the Popes who held and applied the Council—Pope John, Pope Paul. Let us try to improve the Church by becoming better ourselves. Each of us and the whole Church could recite the prayer I am accustomed to recite: "Lord, take me as I am, with my defects, with my shortcomings, but make me become as You want me to be."

I must say a word also to our dear sick, whom I see there. You know, Jesus said: "I hide behind them; what is done for them is done for me." So we venerate the Lord Himself in their persons and we hope that the Lord will be close to them, and help and sustain them.

On our right, on the other hand, there are the newlyweds. They have received a great sacrament. Let us wish that this sacrament which they have received will really bring not only goods of this world, but more spiritual graces. Last century there was in France a great professor, Frederick Ozanam. He taught at the Sorbonne, and was so eloquent, so capable! His friend was Lacordaire, who said: "He is so gifted, he is so good, he will become a priest, he will become a great bishop, this fellow!" No! He met a nice girl and they got married. Lacordaire was disappointed and said: "Poor Ozanam! He too has fallen into the trap!" But two years later, Lacordaire came to Rome, and was received by Pius IX. "Come, come, Father," he said. "I have always heard that Jesus established seven sacraments. Now you come along and change everything. You tell me that He established six sacraments, and a trap! No, Father, marriage is not a trap — it is a great sacrament!"

So let us express again our best wishes for these dear newlyweds: may the Lord bless them!

"Dear Young People"

Angelus Message, September 17, 1978.

Next Tuesday, nearly twelve million boys and girls go back to school. The Pope hopes he is not interfering unduly in Minister Pedini's job if he extends his heartiest good wishes both to teachers and to scholars.

Italian teachers have behind them classic examples of exemplary attachment and dedication to the school. Giosuè Carducci was a professor at Bologna University. He went to Florence for certain celebrations. One evening he took leave of the Minister of Education. "No," the Minister said, "stay tomorrow, too."

"I can't, Your Excellency. Tomorrow I have a lecture at the university and the students are waiting for me."

"I dispense you."

"You may dispense me, but I don't." Professor Carducci had really a high sense both of the school and of the pupils. He was of the race of those who say: "To teach John Latin, it is not enough to know Latin, one must also know and love John." And again: "The value of the lesson depends on the preparation."

I would like to remind the pupils of the primary school of their friend Pinocchio: not the one who played truant one day to go and see the puppets; but the other one, the Pinocchio who took a liking to school, to such an extent that every day, for the whole academic year, he was the first to enter the classroom and the last to leave it. My most affectionate wishes, however, go to pupils of the secondary schools, especially senior ones. They have not only the immediate problems of the school, but looming up in the distance is their life when they leave school. Both in Italy and in other nations of the world today, the doors are wide open for those who wish to enter the secondary schools and the universities. But when they have their diploma or their degree and leave school, they are only little, little fledglings, and they cannot find work, and they cannot get married. These are problems that the society of today must really study and try to solve.

The Pope, too, was a pupil of these schools: junior high school, senior high school, university. But I was thinking only of youth and the parish. No one came to tell me: "You will become Pope." Oh! If only they had told me! If they had told me, I would have studied more, I would have prepared myself. Now, on the contrary, I am old—there is no time.

But you, dear young people, who are studying, you are really young, you have time, you have youth, health, memory and brains: try to exploit all these things. The ruling class of tomorrow is about to come out of your schools. Some of you will become ministers, members of Parliament, senators, mayors, councillors, or else engineers, head physicians—you will occupy posts in society. And he who occupies a post must have the necessary competence; he must prepare himself. General Wellington, the man who defeated Napoleon, made a point of returning to England to see the military college where he had studied, where he had prepared himself, and he said to the cadets: "Look, the battle of Waterloo was won here." And so I say to you, dear boys and girls: you will have battles in life at the age of 30, 40, 50; but if you want to win them, you must begin now, prepare now, be assiduous in study and at school now.

Let us pray to the Lord to help teachers, pupils and also the families that are looking at the school with the same affection and with the same concern as the Pope.

The Virtue
of Christian Hope

To a General Audience, September 20, 1978.

The second of the seven "Lamps of Sanctification" for Pope John was hope. Today I will speak to you of this virtue, which is obligatory for every Christian. In his *Paradiso* (cantos 24, 25 and 26), Dante imagined himself taking an examination in Christianity. A magnificent commission was operating. "Do you have faith?" St. Peter asks him first. "Do you have hope?" St. James continues. "Do you have charity?" St. John ends. "Yes," Dante answers. "I have faith, I have hope, I have charity." He proves it and passes with full marks.

I said that hope is obligatory: that does not mean that hope is ugly or hard. On the contrary, anyone who lives it travels in an atmosphere of trust and abandonment, saying with the psalmist: "Lord, You are my rock, my shield, my fortress, my refuge, my lamp, my shepherd, my salvation. Even if an army were to encamp against me, my heart will not fear; and if the battle rises against me, even then I am confident."

THREE TRUTHS

You will say: is not this psalmist exaggeratedly enthusiastic? Is it possible that things always went right for him? No, they did not always go right. He, too, knows, and says so, that the bad are often fortunate and the good oppressed. He even complained to the Lord about it sometimes; he went so far as to say: "Why are You sleeping, Lord? Why are You silent? Wake up, listen to me, Lord." But his hope remained: firm, unshakeable. To him and to all those who hope can be applied what St. Paul said of Abraham: "In hope he believed against hope" (Rom. 4:18).

You will say further: how can this happen? It happens because one is attached to three truths: God is almighty, God loves me immensely, God is faithful to promises. And it is He, the God of mercy, who kindles trust in me; so that I do not feel lonely, or useless, or abandoned, but involved in a destiny of salvation, which will lead to Paradise one day. I mentioned the Psalms. The same certain confidence vibrates in the books of the saints. I would like you to read a homily delivered by St. Augustine on Easter day about *Alleluia*. We will sing the true *Alleluia* — he says, approximately — in Paradise. That will be the *Alleluia* of full love: this one, now, is the *Alleluia* of starving love, that is, of hope.

Someone will say: what if I am a poor sinner? I reply to him as I replied to an unknown lady, who had confessed to me many years ago. She was discouraged because, she said, she had a stormy life morally. "May I ask you," I said, "how old you are?"

"Thirty-five."

"Thirty-five! But you can live for another forty or fifty years and do a great deal of good. So, repentant as you are, instead of thinking of the past, project yourself into the future and renew your life, with God's help."

OUR IMPERFECTIONS

On that occasion I quoted St. Francis de Sales, who speaks of "our dear imperfections." I explained: God detests failings because they are failings. On the other hand, however, in a certain sense He loves failings since they give to Him an opportunity to show His mercy and to us an opportunity to remain humble and to understand and to sympathize with our neighbor's failings.

Not everyone shares this sympathy of mine for hope. Nietzsche, for example, calls it the "virtue of the weak." According to him, it makes the Christian a useless, separated, resigned person, extraneous to the progress of the world. Others speak of "alienation," which, they say, turns the Christian away from the struggle for human advancement. But "the Christian message," the Council said, "far from deterring men from the task of building up the world ... binds them, rather, to all this by a still more stringent obligation" (*Gaudium et Spes*, n. 34, cf. nn. 39 and 7 and "Message to the World" of the Council Fathers on October 20, 1962).

In the course of the centuries there have also appeared from time to time affirmations and tendencies of Christians that were too pessimistic with regard to man. But these affirmations were disapproved of by the Church and were forgotten, thanks to a host of joyful and hard-working saints, to Christian humanism, to the ascetic teachers, whom Saint-Beuve called "les doux," and to a comprehensive theology. Şt. Thomas Aquinas, for example, puts among the virtues *jucunditas,* or the capacity of changing things heard and seen into a cheerful smile — to the extent and in the way appropriate (cf. 2. *2ae*, q. 168, a.2). This kind of cheerfulness, I explained to my pupils, was shown by that Irish mason who fell from the scaffolding and broke his legs. He was taken to the hospital and the doctor and sister nurse

"St. Thomas Aquinas puts among the virtues the capacity of changing things heard and seen into a cheerful smile."

John Paul I

rushed to him. "Poor thing," the latter said, "you hurt yourself falling." But the patient said: "Mother, not exactly falling, but reaching the ground I hurt myself."

JOY IN OUR LIFE

When St. Thomas declared that joking and making people smile was a virtue, he was in agreement with the "glad tidings" preached by Christ, and with the *hilaritas* recommended by St. Augustine. He overcame pessimism, clothed Christian life in joy and invited us to keep up our courage also with the healthy, pure joys which we meet on our way.

When I was a boy, I read something about Andrew Carnegie, the Scot who went to America with his parents and gradually became one of the richest men in the world. He was not a Catholic, but I was struck by the fact that he returned insistently to the simple, true joys of his life. "I was born in poverty," he said, "but I would not exchange the memories of my childhood with those of a millionaire's children. What do they know of family joys, of the sweet figure of a mother who combines the duties of nurse, washerwoman, cook, teacher, angel and saint?" When still very young, he took a job in a Pittsburgh mill with 56 miserable lire a month as wages. One evening, instead of giving him his wage at once, the cashier told him to wait. Carnegie was trembling: "Now they'll dismiss me." On the contrary, after paying the others, the cashier said to him: "Andrew, I've watched your work carefully; I've come to the conclusion that it is worth more than that of the others. I'm raising your wage to sixty-seven lire." Carnegie said many years afterwards, "All my millions put together never gave me the joy of that eleven lire raise."

Certainly, these joys, though good and encouraging, must not be absolutized. They are something, not everything; they serve as a means, they are not the supreme purpose; they do not last forever, but only for a short time. "Christians," St. Paul wrote, "deal with the world as though they had no dealings with it. For the form of this world is passing away" (cf. 1 Cor. 7:31). Christ had already said: "Seek first of all the kingdom of God" (Mt. 6:33).

THE CHURCH MUST ALSO HUMANIZE

In conclusion, I would like to refer to a hope which is proclaimed Christian by some people, and on the contrary is Christian only up to a certain point. Let me explain. At the Council, I, too, voted for the "Message to the World" of the Council Fathers. In it we said: the principal task of divinizing does not exempt the Church from the task of *human-*

izing. I voted for *Gaudium et Spes.* I was moved and enthusiastic when *Populorum Progressio* came out. I think that the magisterium of the Church will never sufficiently insist on presenting and recommending the solution of the great problems of freedom, justice, peace, development; and Catholic laity will never fight sufficiently to solve these problems. It is wrong, on the other hand, to state that political, economic and social liberation coincides with salvation in Jesus Christ, that the *Regnum Dei* is identified with the *Regnum hominis,* that *Ubi Lenin ibi Jerusalem.*

In the last few days the subject "the future of hope" has been dealt with at Freiburg, in the eighty-fifth Katholikentag. They were speaking of the "world" to be improved, and the word "future" was right. But if we pass from hope for the "world" to hope for individual souls, then we must speak also of "eternity." On the seashore at Ostia, in a famous conversation, Augustine and Monica, "forgetting the past and turning to the future, asked themselves what eternal life would be" *(Confess. I, n. 10).* This is Christian hope; this is what Pope John intended and what we intend when we pray, with the catechism: "My God, I hope from Your goodness...eternal life and the necessary graces to deserve it with good works, which I must do and want to do. My God, let me not remain confounded forever."

The Christian Family: a Community of Love

To Archbishops and Bishops of the U.S. Twelfth Pastoral Region, on the occasion of their "ad limina" visit, September 21, 1978.

Dear Brothers in Christ,

It is a real pleasure for us to meet, for the first time, a group of American bishops making their *ad limina* visit. With all our heart we welcome you; we want you to feel at home, to feel the joy of being together in the family. Our great desire at this time is to confirm you all in your faith and in your service to God's people; we want to keep alive the ministry of Peter in the Church.

Since becoming Pope, we have studied with particular attention the wise teaching that our beloved predecessor, Paul VI, gave earlier this year to the United States' Ministry of Reconciliation on promoting life, and on fostering devotion to the Eucharist. His teaching is ours; and we renew the encouragement and guidance that he gave you in those discourses.

POWER OF THE FAMILY

Although we are new in the pontificate — just a beginner — we too want to choose topics that deeply touch the life of the Church and that will be very relevant to your episcopal ministry. We believe that the Christian family is a good place to start. The Christian family is so important, and its role is so basic in transforming the world and in building up the kingdom of God, that the Council called it a "domestic Church" *(Lumen Gentium,* n. 11).

Let us never grow tired of proclaiming the family as a community of love: conjugal love unites the couple and is procreative of new life; it mirrors the divine love, is communicated, and, in the words of *Gaudium et Spes,* is actually a sharing in the covenant of love of Christ and His Church (n. 48). We were all given the great grace of being born into such a community of love; it will be easy for us to uphold its value.

And then we must encourage parents in their role as educators of their children — the first catechists and the best ones. What a great task and challenge they have: to teach children the love of God, to make it something real for them. And by God's grace, how easily some families can fulfill the role of being a *primum seminarium (Optatam Totius,* n. 2); the germ of a vocation to the priesthood is nourished through family prayer, the example of faith and the support of love.

TIMELY TOPICS

What a wonderful thing it is when families realize the power they have for the sanctification of the world; the mutual sanctification of husband and wife and the reciprocal influence between parents and children. And then, by the loving witness of their lives, families can bring Christ's Gospel to others. A vivid realization of the sharing of the laity—and especially the family— in the salvific mission of the Church is one of the greatest legacies of the Second Vatican Council. We can never thank God enough for this gift.

It is up to us to keep this realization strong, by supporting and defending the family—each and every family. Our own ministry is so vital: to preach the word of God and to celebrate the sacraments. It is from them that our people draw their strength and joy. Ours too is the role of encouraging families to fidelity to the law of God and the Church. We need never fear to proclaim all the exigencies of God's word, for Christ is with us and says today as before: "He who hears you, hears me" (Lk. 10:16). In particular, the indissolubility of Christian marriage is important; although it is a difficult part of our message, we must proclaim it faithfully as part of God's word, part of the mystery of faith. At the same time we are close to our people in their problems and difficulties. They must always know that we love them.

Today we want to express our admiration and praise for all the efforts being made to guard and preserve the family as God made it, as God wants it. All over the world Christian families are trying to fulfill their wonderful calling and we are close to all of them. And priests and religious are trying to support and assist them—and all these efforts are worthy of the greatest praise. Our special support goes to those who help couples preparing for Christian marriage by offering them the full teaching of the Church and by encouraging them in the highest ideals of the Christian family. We wish to add a particular word of praise also for those, especially priests, who work so generously and devotedly in ecclesiastical tribunals, in fidelity to the doctrine of the Church, to safeguard the marriage bond, to give witness to its indissolubility in accordance with the teaching of Jesus, and to assist families in need.

RENEWAL THROUGH
FAMILY PRAYER

The holiness of the Christian family is indeed a most apt means for producing the serene renewal of the Church which the Council so eagerly desired. Through family prayer, the *ecclesia domestica* becomes an effective reality and leads to the transformation of the world. And all the efforts of parents to instill God's love into their children and to support them by the example of faith constitute a most relevant apostolate for the twentieth century. Parents with special problems are worthy of our particular pastoral care, and all our love.

Dear Brothers, we want you to know where our priorities lie. Let us do everything we can for the Christian family, so that our people may fulfill their great vocation in Christian joy and share intimately and effectively in the Church's mission—Christ's mission—of salvation. And be assured that you yourselves have our full support in the love of the Lord Jesus, and we give you all our apostolic blessing.

The True Christian Community

On September 23, 1978, Pope John Paul I took possession of his cathedral as Bishop of Rome. This is the Arch-basilica of St. John Lateran. After the Gospel of the Mass, which followed the ceremony of taking possession, the Pope delivered the following homily:

Heartfelt thanks to the Cardinal Vicar for the delicate words with which—in the name of the Episcopal Council, the Chapter of the Lateran, the clergy, the men and women religious, and of the faithful—he decided to express the devotion and the intentions of effective collaboration in the diocese of Rome. The first concrete evidence of this collaboration is the immense sum placed at my disposal in order to provide with a church and a parochial structure a peripheral area of the city hitherto deprived of this essential community help for the Christian life. Truly touched, I thank you.

The Master of Ceremonies has chosen the three lessons for this solemn liturgy. He has judged them suitable, and I wish to explain them to you. The *first lesson* (Is. 60:16) can be referred to Rome. Everyone knows that the Pope acquires authority over the whole Church inasmuch as he is Bishop of Rome, that is, successor of Peter in this city. Thanks especially to Peter, the Jerusalem of which Isaiah spoke can be considered a figure, a foretelling of Rome. Of Rome, too, inasmuch as it is the See of Peter, the place of his martyrdom and the center of the Catholic Church, it can be said: "the Lord will arise upon you, and his glory will be seen...the nations shall come to your light" (Is. 60:2). Recalling the pilgrimages of the Holy Year and those that continue with a constant flow during the normal years, one can, with the prophet, address Rome as follows: "Lift up your eyes round about and see;...your sons shall come from afar...the abundance of the sea shall be turned to you, the wealth of the nations shall come to you" (Is. 60:4, 5). This is an honor for the Bishop of Rome and for you all. But it is also a responsibility. Shall the pilgrims find here a model of a true Christian community? With the help of God shall we, bishop and faithful, be able to cause to come true here the words of Isaiah, written under those first cited, namely: "Violence shall no more be heard in your land... your people shall all be righteous" (Is. 10:18, 21)?

A few moments ago, Professor Argan, Syndic of Rome, made me a courteous address of greetings and good wishes. Some words of his caused me to think of one of the prayers that I recited as a child with Mamma. It went like this: "The sins that cry for vengeance in the presence of God are...to oppress the poor, to defraud the workers of a just wage." In his turn, the parish priest questioned me at school on the catechism: "Why are the sins that cry for vengeance in the presence of God among the more grievous and harmful?" *Reply:* "...Because they are directly contrary to the good of mankind and are most hateful inasmuch as, more than others, they provoke the chastisements of God" (*Catechism of Pius X,* n. 154).

Rome will be a true Christian community if God is honored by you not merely with a multitude of the faithful in the churches, not merely with private life that is lived morally, but also with love for the poor. These, the Roman deacon Lawrence said, are the true treasures of the Church. They must be helped, however, by those who can, to have more and to be more, without becoming humiliated and offended by ostentatious riches, by money squandered on futile things and not invested — insofar as is possible — in enterprises of advantage to all.

The *second lesson* (Heb. 13:7-8; 15-17; 20-21) can be applied to the faithful of Rome.

As I have said, the Master of Ceremonies has chosen it. I confess that when it speaks of obedience it places me in a slight embarrassment. Today, when personal human rights are confronted with the rights of authority and of the law, it is so difficult to convince! In the Book of Job there is a description of a war-horse: he leaps like a locust and snorts; he paws the ground with his hoof, then he hurls himself fiercely forward; when the trumpet sounds he neighs with delight; he smells the battle from afar, the cries of the captains and the noise of the troops (cf. Job 39:10-25) — the symbol of liberty. Authority, on the contrary, is like the prudent rider: he mounts the horse and, now with gentle voice, now making judicious use of the spurs, of the bridle and of the whip, he urges it on or controls its impetuous course, curbs it and restrains it. To reconcile the horse and the rider — liberty and authority — has become a social problem.

It is likewise with the Church. At the Council there was an attempt to resolve it in the fourth chapter of *Lumen Gentium*. Here are the conciliar indications for the "rider": "The sacred pastors know very well how much the laity contribute to the welfare of the whole Church. They know that they themselves were not established by Christ to undertake alone the whole salvific mission of the Church to the world, but that it is their exalted office to be shepherds of the faithful and to recognize the latter's contribution and charisms in such a way that all, in their measure, will with one mind cooperate in the common task" (*Lumen Gentium,* n. 30). Further, the pastors are also aware that "in the decisive battles it is at times from the front that the happiest initiatives begin" (*Lumen Gentium,* n. 37, note 7). On the other hand, here is a conciliar indication for the "high-spirited war-horse," that is, for the laity: "the faithful should acquiesce to the bishop as the Church to Jesus Christ and as Jesus Christ to the Father" (*Lumen Gentium,* n. 27). Let us pray that the Lord will aid both the bishop and the faithful, both the rider and the horses.

It has been said to me that in the diocese of Rome there are numerous persons who devote themselves to the faithful, numerous catechists; many also await a signal to intervene and to collaborate. May the Lord help us all to build at Rome a living and active Christian community. It is not pointlessly that I have quoted the fourth chapter of *Lumen Gentium:* it is the chapter on "ecclesial communion." What has been said, however, has special reference to the laity. The priests, the men and women religious, have a special position, bound as they are either to the promise or to the vow of obedience. I recall, as one of the solemn points of my existence, the moment in which, with my hands in those of the bishop, I said: "I promise." From that time, I considered myself bound for my whole life, and never have I thought that it was a matter of an unimportant ceremony. I hope that the priests of Rome think likewise. To them and to the religious St. Francis de Sales would recall the example of St. John the Baptist who lived in the desert, far from the Lord, yet so greatly desiring to be near to Him. Why? Through obedience: "He knew," writes the saint, "that to find the Lord outside of obedience meant to lose Him" (F. de Sales, *Oeuvres*, Annecy, 1806, p. 321).

The *third lesson* (Mt. 28:16-20) reminds the Bishop of Rome of his duties. The first is to teach, proposing the Lord's word with fidelity both to God and to the listeners; with humility, but with fearless sincerity.

Among my holy predecessors, bishops of Rome, there are two who are also Doctors of the Church: St. Leo, conqueror of Attila, and St. Gregory the Great. In the writings of the first are very high theological thought and a sparkling Latin style that is marvelously designed; I do not think that I could imitate him, not even from afar. The second, in his books, is "like a father who instructs his children and sets them apart out of his solicitude for their eternal salvation" (I. Schuster, *Liber Sacramentorum*, vol. 1, Turin

1920, p. 46). I would like to try to imitate the second, who dedicates the entire third book of his *Regula Pastoralis* to the theme of how teaching should be done, that is, how the pastor should instruct.

For forty whole chapters Gregory indicates in a concrete way various forms of instruction according to the various circumstances of social conditions, age, health, and moral temperament of the hearers. Poor and rich, cheerful and melancholic, superiors and subjects, learned and ignorant, cheeky and shy, and so forth; all are there in this book—it is like the valley of Jehoshaphat. At the Second Vatican Council, there was a seemingly new thing which came to be called "pastoral approach," not indeed that which was taught to the pastors, but that which the pastors did to face up to the needs, the anxieties, the hopes of men.

This "new" approach had already been applied many centuries earlier by Gregory, both in preaching and in the government of the Church.

The second duty, expressed in the word "baptize," refers to the sacraments and to the whole of the liturgy. The diocese of Rome has followed the program of the CEI: "Evangelization and Sacraments." It already knows that evangelization, sacraments, and holy life are three moments on the one course: evangelization prepares for the sacrament, the sacrament draws him who has received it to live in a Christian way. I should like this great concept to be applied in ever-increasing measure. I should like also that Rome should in fact give a good example of liturgy celebrated devoutly and without ill-placed "creativity." Certain abuses in liturgical matters have succeeded, through reaction, in favoring attitudes that have led to a taking up of positions that in themselves cannot be upheld and are in contrast with the Gospel. In appealing with affection and with hope to the sense of responsibility of everyone, before God and the Church, I should like to be able to give an assurance that every liturgical irregularity will be diligently avoided.

And now I have come to the last episcopal duty: "to teach and to observe"; it is the *diaconia*, the service of guiding and governing. Although already for twenty years I have been Bishop at Vittorio Veneto and at Venice, I admit that I have not yet "learned the job" well. At Rome I shall put myself in the school of St. Gregory the Great who writes: "[the pastor] should, with compassion, be close to each one who is subject to him; forgetful of his rank he should consider himself on a level with the good subjects, but he should not fear to exercise the rights of his authority against the wicked. Remember: while every subject lifts up

"...I can assure you that I love you, that
I desire only to enter into your service and
to place the poor powers that I have, however
little they are, at the disposal of all."

John Paul I

to heaven that which he has done well, no one dares to censure that which he has done badly; when he puts down vices he does not cease, with humility, to recognize himself as on the level of the brother whom he has corrected; and he considers that he is all the more a debtor before God, inasmuch as his actions remain unpunished before men" (*Reg. Past.*, Part Two, cc. 5 and 6 *passim*).

The explanation of the lessons ends here. Let me add only one more thing: it is God's law that one cannot do good to anyone if one does not first of all wish him well. On account of this, St. Pius V, on becoming Patriarch of Venice, exclaimed in San Marco: "What would become of me, Venetians, if I did not love you?" I say something similar: I can assure you that I love you, that I desire only to enter into your service and to place the poor powers that I have, however little they are, at the disposal of all.

Fidelity to Christian Ideals

Address to the City Council and Mayor of Rome, September 23, 1978.

Mr. Mayor,

I am deeply grateful to you for these respectful and sincere expressions which, on behalf of the Municipal Government and all the citizens of Rome, you have kindly addressed to me on my way from the Vatican residence to the Cathedral of St. John Lateran.

This intermediate stop at the foot of the Capitol hill has a special significance for me not only because of the host of historical memories which intermingle here and which concern both civil Rome and Christian Rome, but also because it enables me to have a first, direct contact with those in charge of civic life and of its sound organization. It is, therefore, a propitious opportunity to extend to them my cordial greeting and good wishes.

The problems of Rome, to which you referred with motivated concern, find me particularly attentive and sensitive because of their urgency, their seriousness and, above all, the hardships and human and family dramas of which they are not infrequently the manifest sign. As bishop of the city, which is the original See of the pastoral ministry entrusted to me, I feel these painful experiences more acutely reflected in my heart, and am urged by them to availability, collaboration and to that contribution of a moral and spiritual nature, corresponding to the specific nature of my service, in order to be able at least to relieve them. I say this not only in a personal capacity, but also on behalf of the sons of the Church of God here in Rome: of the bishops, my collaborators; the priests and religious; members of the Catholic associations; and the individual faithful engaged in various ways in pastoral, educational, charitable and scholastic action.

The hope which I heard with pleasure echoed in your kind address is for us believers — as I recalled at the General Audience last Wednesday — an obligatory virtue and an elect gift of God. May it serve to reawaken energies and resolutions in each of us and, as I trust, in all fellow citizens of good will; may it serve to inspire initiatives and programs, in order that those problems may have a suitable solution and Rome may remain faithful, in actual fact, to those unmistakably Christian ideals which are called hunger and thirst for justice, an active contribution for peace, the superior dignity of human work, respect and love for brothers, and unfailing solidarity with regard to the weakest.

Not Violence, but Love, Can Do Everything!

Angelus Message, September 24, 1978.

Yesterday afternoon I went to St. John Lateran. Thanks to the Romans, to the kindness of the Mayor and some authorities of the Italian government, it was a joyful moment for me.

On the contrary, it was not joyful but painful to learn from the newspapers a few days ago that a Roman student had been killed for a trivial reason, in cold blood. It is one of the many cases of violence which are continually afflicting this poor and restless society of ours.

The case of Luca Locci, a seven-year-old boy kidnapped three months ago, has come up again in the last few days. People sometimes say: "We are in a society that is all rotten, all dishonest." That is not true. There are still so many good people, so many honest people. Rather, what can be done to improve society? I would say: let each of us try to be good and to infect others with a goodness imbued with the meekness and love taught by Christ. Christ's golden rule was: "Do not do to others what you do not want done to yourself. Do to others what you want done to yourself." And He always gave. Put on the cross, not only did He forgive those who crucified Him, but He excused them. He said: "Father, forgive them for they know not what they do." This is Christianity; these are sentiments which, if put into practice, would help society so much.

This year is the thirtieth anniversary of the death of Georges Bernanos, a great Catholic writer. One of his best-known works is *Dialogues of the Carmelites*. It was published a year after his death. He had prepared it working on a story of the German authoress, Gertrud von Le Fort. He had prepared it for the theater.

It went on the stage. It was set to music and then shown on the screens of the whole world. It became extremely well known. The fact, however, was a historical one. Pius X, in 1906, right here in Rome, had beatified the sixteen Carmelites of Compiègne, martyrs during the French Revolution. During the trial they were condemned "to death for fanaticism." And one of them asked in her simplicity: "Your Honor, what does fanaticism mean?" And the judge: "It is your foolish membership of religion." "Oh, Sisters," she then said, "did you hear, we are condemned for our attachment to faith. What happiness to die for Jesus Christ!"

They were brought out of the prison of the Conciergerie, and made to climb into the fatal cart. On the way they sang hymns; when they reached the guillotine, one after the other knelt before the Prioress and renewed the vow of obedience. Then they struck up "Veni Creator"; the song, however, became weaker and weaker, as the heads of the poor sisters fell, one by one, under the guillotine. The Prioress, Sister Teresa of St. Augustine, was the last, and her last words were the following: "Love will always be victorious; love can do everything." That was the right word: not violence, but love can do everything.

Let us ask the Lord for the grace that a new wave of love for our neighbor may sweep over this poor world.

Golden Jubilee

On the occasion of the fiftieth anniversary of his ordination to the priesthood, His Eminence Cardinal Siri, Archbishop of Genoa, received the following telegram of good wishes from Pope John Paul I.

As with spiritual joy you recall the fiftieth anniversary of your priesthood, venerable Brother, we are present with you in spirit, congratulating you; acknowledging with praise the work that you have done in this space of time for the glory of God, the honor of the Church, the salvation of souls; asking heavenly gifts for you. These wishes are strengthened by the apostolic blessing which we most lovingly bestow on you and also wish to extend to the auxiliary bishop, clergy and faithful committed to your care.

"We Must Make Progress in Love!"

To a General Audience, September 27, 1978.

"My God, with all my heart, above all things I love You, infinite good and our eternal happiness, and for Your sake I love my neighbor as myself and forgive offenses received. Oh Lord, may I love You more and more." This is a very well-known prayer, embellished with biblical phrases. My mother taught it to me. I recite it several times a day even now, and I will try to explain it to you, word by word, as a parish catechist would do.

We are at Pope John's "third lamp of sanctification": charity. *I love*. In the philosophy class the teacher would say to me: "You know St. Mark's bell tower? You do? That means that it has somehow entered your mind: physically it has remained where it was, but within you it has imprinted almost an intellectual portrait of itself. Do you, on the other hand, *love* St. Mark's bell tower?

That means that portrait, from within, pushes you and bends you, almost carries you, makes you go in your mind towards the bell tower which is outside. In a word: to love means traveling, rushing with one's heart towards the object loved." The *Imitation of Christ* says: he who loves "*currit, volat, laetatur*," runs, flies and rejoices (1. III, c. V, n. 4).

JOURNEY OF THE HEART

To love God is therefore a journeying with one's heart to God. A wonderful journey! When I was a boy, I was thrilled by the journeys described by Jules Verne (*Twenty Thousand Leagues Under the Sea, From the Earth to the Moon, 'Round the World in Eighty Days,* etc.). But the journeys of love for God are far more interesting. You read them in the lives of the saints. St. Vincent de Paul, whose feast we celebrate today, for example, is a giant of charity: he loved God more than a father and a mother, and he himself was a father for prisoners, sick people, orphans and the poor. St. Peter Claver, dedicating himself entirely to God, used to sign: *Peter, the slave of the negroes forever.*

The journey also brings sacrifices, but these must not stop us. Jesus is on the cross: you want to kiss Him? You cannot help bending over the cross and letting yourself be pricked by some thorns of the crown which is on the Lord's head (cf. Sales, *Oeuvres,* Annecy, t. XXI, p. 153). You cannot cut the figure of good St. Peter, who had no difficulty in shouting, "Long live Jesus" on Mount Tabor, where there was joy, but did not even let himself be seen beside Jesus at Mount Calvary, where there was risk and suffering (cf. Sales, *Oeuvres,* t. XV, p. 140).

Love for God is also a mysterious journey: that is, I cannot start unless God takes the initiative first. "No one," Jesus said, "can come to me, unless the Father who sent me draws him" (Jn 6:44). St. Augustine asked himself: but what about human freedom? God, however, who willed and constructed this freedom, knows how to respect it, though bringing hearts to the point He intended: *"parum est voluntate, etiam voluptate traheris";* God draws you not only in a way that you yourself want, but even in such a way that you enjoy being drawn (Augustinus, *In Io. Evang.* Tr. 26, 4).

"ALL MY HEART"

With all my heart. I stress, here, the adjective "all." Totalitarianism, in politics, is an ugly thing. In religion, on the contrary, a totalitarianism on our side towards God is a very good thing. It is written: "You shall love the Lord your God with all your heart, and with all your soul, and with all your might. And these words which I command you this day shall be upon your heart; and you shall teach them diligently to your children, and shall talk of them when you sit in your house, and when you walk by the way, and when you lie down, and when you rise. And you shall bind them as a sign upon your hand, and they shall be as frontlets between your eyes. And you shall write them on the doorposts of your house and on your gates" (Deut. 6:5-9). That "all" repeated and applied insistently is really the banner of Christian maximalism. And it is right: God is too great, He deserves too much from us for us to be able to throw to Him, as to a poor Lazarus, a few crumbs of our time and our heart. He is infinite good and will be our eternal happiness: money, pleasure, the fortunes of this world, compared with Him, are just fragments of good and fleeting moments of happiness. It would not be wise to give so much of ourselves to these things and little of ourselves to Jesus.

BOTH GOD AND MAN

Above everything else. Now we come to a direct comparison between God and man, between God and the world. It would not be right to say: "Either God or man." We must love "both God and man"; the latter, however, never more than God or against God or as much as God. In other words: love of God, though prevalent, is not exclusive. The Bible declares Jacob holy (Dn. 3:35) and loved by God (Mal. 1:2; Rom. 9:13); it shows him working for seven years to win Rachel as his wife; "and they seemed to him but a few days because of the love he had for her" (Gn. 29:20). Francis de Sales makes a little comment on these words: "Jacob," he writes, "loves Rachel with all his might, and he loves God with all his might; but he does not therefore love Rachel as God nor God as Rachel. He loves God as his God above all things and more than himself; he loves Rachel as his wife above all other women and as himself. He loves God with absolutely and superbly supreme love, and Rachel with supreme husbandly love; one love is not contrary to the other because love of Rachel does not violate the supreme advantages of love of God" (*Oeuvres*, t. V, p. 175).

LOVE OF NEIGHBOR

And for your sake I love my neighbor. Here we are in the presence of two loves which are "twin brothers" and inseparable. It is easy to love some persons; difficult to love others; we do not find them likeable, they have offended us and hurt us; only if

I love God in earnest can I love them as sons of God and because He asks me to. Jesus also established how to love one's neighbor: that is, not only with feeling, but with facts. This is the way, He said. I will ask you: I was hungry in the person of my humbler brothers, did you give me food? Did you visit me when I was sick? (cf. Mt. 25:34ff.)

The catechism puts these and other words of the Bible in the double list of the seven corporal works of mercy and the seven spiritual ones. The list is not complete and it would be necessary to update it. Among the starving, for example, today, it is no longer a question just of this or that individual; there are whole peoples.

We all remember the great words of Pope Paul VI: "Today the peoples in hunger are making a dramatic appeal to the peoples blessed with abundance. The Church shudders at this cry of anguish and calls each one to give a loving response of charity to this brother's cry for help" (Populorum Progressio, n. 3). At this point justice is added to charity, because Paul VI says also, "Private property does not constitute for anyone an absolute and unconditioned right. No one is justified in keeping for his exclusive use what he does not need, when others lack necessities" (Populorum Progressio, n. 23). Consequently "every exhausting armaments race becomes an intolerable scandal" (*Populorum Progressio*, n. 53).

In the light of these strong expressions it can be seen how far we — individuals and peoples — still are from loving others "as ourselves," as Jesus commanded.

Another commandment: *I forgive offenses received*. It almost seems that the Lord gives precedence to this forgiveness over worship: "So if you are offering your gift at the altar, and there remember that your brother has something against you, leave your gift there before the altar and go; first be reconciled to your brother, and then come and offer your gift" (Mt. 5:23-24).

THIRST FOR PROGRESS

The last words of the prayer are: *Lord, may I love You more and more*. Here, too, there is obedience to a commandment of God, who put thirst for progress in our hearts. From pile-dwellings, caves and the first huts we have passed to houses, apartment buildings and skyscrapers; from journeys on foot, on the back of a mule or of a camel, to coaches, trains and airplanes. And people desire to progress further with more and more rapid means of transport, reaching more and more distant goals. But to love God, we have seen, is also a journey: God wants it to be more and more intense and perfect. He said to all His followers:

"You are the light of the world, the salt of the earth" (Mt. 5:13-14); "You must be perfect as your heavenly Father is perfect" (Mt. 5:48). That means: to love God not a little, but so much; not to stop at the point at which we have arrived, but with His help, to progress in love.

The Challenge of Evangelization

To Cardinal Julio Rosales, Archbishop of Cebu, with a group of bishops from the Philippines who were making their "ad limina" visit, September 28, 1978.

Dear Brothers in Christ,

In welcoming you with deep affection, we wish to recall a passage found in the Breviary. This passage has struck us forcefully. It concerns Christ, and was spoken by Paul VI on his visit to the Philippines: "I must bear witness to His name: Jesus is the Christ, the Son of the living God... He is the king of the new world; He is the secret of history; He is the key to our destiny" (13th Sunday of the Year: homily of November 29, 1970).

On our part we hope to sustain you, support you, and encourage you in the great mission of the episcopate: to proclaim Jesus Christ and to evangelize His people.

Among the rights of the faithful, one of the greatest is the right to receive God's word in all its entirety and purity, with all its exigencies and power. A great challenge of our day is the full evangelization of all those who have been baptized. In this, the bishops of the Church have a prime responsibility. Our message must be a clear proclamation of salvation in Jesus Christ. With Peter we must say to Christ, in the presence of our people: "You have the words of eternal life" (Jn. 6:69).

IN JESUS' NAME

For us, evangelization involves an explicit teaching about the name of Jesus, His identity, His teaching, His kingdom and His promises. And His chief promise is eternal life. Jesus truly has words that lead us to eternal life.

Just recently at a general audience, we spoke to the faithful about eternal life. We are convinced that it is necessary for us to emphasize this element, in order to complete our message and to model our teaching on that of Jesus.

From the days of the Gospel, and in imitation of the Lord, who "went about doing good" (Acts 10:38), the Church is irrevocably committed to contributing to the relief of physical misery and need. But her pastoral charity would be incomplete if she did not point out even "higher needs." In the Philippines Paul VI did precisely this. At a moment when he chose to speak about the poor, about justice and peace, about human rights, about economic and social liberation — at a moment when he also effectively committed the Church to the alleviation of misery — he did not and could not remain silent about the "higher good," the fullness of life in the kingdom of heaven.

More than ever before, we must help our people to realize just how much they need Jesus Christ, the Son of God and the Son of Mary. He is their Savior, the key to their destiny and to the destiny of all humanity.

JUSTICE AND LOVE

Dear Brothers, we are spiritually close to you in all the efforts you are making on behalf of evangelization: as you train catechists, as you promote the biblical apostolate, as you assist and encourage all your priests in their great mission at the service of God's word, and as you lead all your faithful to understand and to fulfill the requirements of justice and Christian love. We greatly esteem these and all your endeavors on behalf of the kingdom of God. In particular, we fully support the affirmation of the missionary vocation, and earnestly hope that it will flourish among your youth.

RADIO VERITAS

We are aware that the Philippines has a great vocation in being the light of Christ in the Far East: to proclaim His truth, His love, His justice and salvation by word and example before its neighbors, the peoples of Asia. We know that you have a privileged instrument in this regard: Radio Veritas. It is our hope that the Philippines will use this great means and every other means to proclaim with the entire Church that Jesus Christ is the Son of God and Savior of the world.

Our greetings go to all your local Churches, especially to the priests and religious. We encourage them to ever greater holiness of life as a condition for the super-natural effectiveness of their apostolate. We love and bless the families of your dioceses and all the laity. We ask the sick and the handicapped to understand their important part in God's plan, and to realize just how much evangelization depends on them.

To all of you, brothers, we impart our special apostolic blessing, invoking upon you joy and strength in Jesus Christ.

Daughters of St. Paul

IN MASSACHUSETTS
    50 St. Paul's Avenue, Boston, Ma. 02130
    172 Tremont Street, Boston, Ma. 02111
IN NEW YORK
    78 Fort Place, Staten Island, N.Y. 10301
    59 East 43rd St., New York, N.Y. 10017
    625 East 187th Street, Bronx, N.Y. 10458
    525 Main Street, Buffalo, N.Y. 14203
IN NEW JERSEY
    Hudson Mall — Route 440 and
        Communipaw Ave., Jersey City, N.J. 07304
IN CONNECTICUT
    202 Fairfield Avenue, Bridgeport, Ct. 06604
IN OHIO
    2105 Ontario St. (at Prospect Ave.), Cleveland, Oh. 44115
    25 E. Eighth Street, Cincinnati, Oh. 45202
IN PENNSYLVANIA
    1719 Chestnut St., Philadelphia, Pa. 19103
IN FLORIDA
    2700 Biscayne Blvd., Miami, Fl. 33137
IN LOUISIANA
    4403 Veterans Memorial Blvd., Metairie, La. 70002
    1800 South Acadian Thruway, P.O. Box 2028,
        Baton Rouge, La. 70802
IN MISSOURI
    1001 Pine St. (at North 10th), St. Louis, Mo. 63101
IN TEXAS
    114 East Main Plaza, San Antonio, Tx. 78205
IN CALIFORNIA
    1570 Fifth Avenue, San Diego, Ca. 92101
    46 Geary Street, San Francisco, Ca. 94108
IN HAWAII
    1143 Bishop St., Honolulu, Hi. 96813
IN ALASKA
    750 West 5th Avenue, Anchorage, Ak. 99501
IN CANADA
    3022 Dufferin Street, Toronto 395, Ontario, Canada
IN ENGLAND
    57, Kensington Church Street, London W. 8, England
IN AUSTRALIA
    58, Abbotsford Rd., Homebush, N.S.W., Sydney 2140,
        Australia